ATLA BIBLIOGRAPHY SERIES
edited by Dr. Kenneth E. Rowe

1. *A Guide to the Study of the Holiness Movement,* by Charles Edwin Jones. 1974.
2. *Thomas Merton: A Bibliography,* by Marquita E. Breit. 1974.
3. *The Sermon on the Mount: A History of Interpretation and Bibliography,* by Warren S. Kissinger. 1975.
4. *The Parables of Jesus: A History of Interpretation and Bibliography,* by Warren S. Kissinger. 1979.
5. *Homosexuality and the Judeo-Christian Tradition: An Annotated Bibliography,* by Thom Horner. 1981.
6. *A Guide to the Study of the Pentecostal Movement,* by Charles Edwin Jones. 1983.
7. *The Genesis of Modern Process Thought: A Historical Outline with Bibliography,* by George R. Lucas, Jr. 1983.
8. *A Presbyterian Bibliography,* by Harold B. Prince. 1983.
9. *Paul Tillich: A Comprehensive Bibliography . . .,* by Richard C. Crossman. 1983.
10. *A Bibliography of the Samaritans,* by Alan David Crown. 1984.
11. *An Annotated and Classified Bibliography of English Literature Pertaining to the Ethiopian Orthodox Church,* by Jon Bonk. 1984.
12. *International Meditation Bibliography, 1950 to 1982,* by Howard R. Jarrell. 1984.
13. *Rabindranath Tagore: A Bibliography,* by Katherine Henn. 1985.
14. *Research in Ritual Studies: A Programmatic Essay and Bibliography,* by Ronald L. Grimes, 1985.
15. *Protestant Theological Education in America,* by Heather F. Day. 1985.
16. *Unconscious: A Guide to Sources,* by Natalino Caputi. 1985.
17. *The New Testament Apocrypha and Pseudepigrapha,* by James H. Charlesworth. 1987.
18. *Black Holiness,* by Charles Edwin Jones. 1987.
19. *A Bibliography on Ancient Ephesus,* by Richard Oster. 1987.
20. *Jerusalem, the Holy City: A Bibliography,* by James D. Purvis. 1987.
21. *An Index to English Periodical Literature on the Old Testament and Ancient Near Eastern Studies,* Volume I, by William G. Hupper. 1987.

A BIBLIOGRAPHY OF ANCIENT EPHESUS

compiled by

RICHARD E. OSTER

ATLA Bibliography Series, No. 19

The American Theological Library Association
and
The Scarecrow Press, Inc.
Metuchen, N.J., & London
1987

Library of Congress Cataloging-in-Publication Data

Oster, Richard.
    A bibliography of ancient Ephesus.

    (ATLA bibliography series ; no. 19)
    Bibliography: p.
    Includes index.
    1. Ephesus (Ancient city)--History--Bibliography.
2. Turkey--Antiquities--Bibliography. 3. Greece--
Antiquities--Bibliography. I. Title. II. Series.
Z2304.E58O87 1987   016.939'23   87-12617
[DF261.E5]
ISBN 0-8108-1996-1

This bibliography is dedicated with greatest affection and esteem to ANNIE MAY ALSTON LEWIS, bibliophile par excellence, for decades of tireless service as Librarian and Faculty member of Harding University Graduate School of Religion.

CONTENTS

EDITOR'S FOREWORD

The American Theological Library Association Bibliography Series is designed to stimulate and encourage the preparation and publication of reliable guides to the literature of religious studies in all its scope and variety. Compilers are free to define their field, make their own selections, and work out internal organization as the unique demands of the subject require. We are pleased to publish Richard Oster's bibliography on Ancient Ephesus as number nineteen in the series.

Mr. Oster studied classical languages and literatures at Texas Tech University in Lubbock, Texas, where he earned the B.A. degree. He took a Master's degree in religious studies at Rice University and completed the doctorate with honors in biblical studies at Princeton Theological Seminary. In addition to a book on The Acts of the Apostles, Mr. Oster has published numerous journal articles. He has taught in the religious studies department at the University of Houston and since 1978 has been professor of New Testament at Harding University Graduate School of Religion in Memphis, Tennessee.

Kenneth E. Rowe
Drew University Library
Madison, N.J.

PREFACE

A brief word about the method used in assembling this bibliography might help the user who wishes to pursue related interests. I, of course, benefited from the early article by L. Bürchner, "Ephesos," in Paulys Realencyclopädie der classischen Altertumswissenschaft 5.2.2773-2822 (1905) as well as the later articles: Wilhelm Alzinger's "Ephesos" (archäologischer Teil), Stefan Karwiese's "Ephesos" (numismatischer Teil), and Dieter Knibbe's "Ephesos" (historisch-epigraphischer Teil), all in Paulys Realencyclopädie der classischen Altertumswissenschaft, Supplementband 12 (1970). Wilhelm Alzinger's Die Stadt des siebenten Weltwunders. Die Wiederentdeckung von Ephesos (1962) was also helpful in tracing the history of the excavations and attendant publications.

Indispensable were such standard bibliographical tools as Archäologische Bibliographie, Fasti Archaeologici, A. M. Mansel, Türkiyenin Arkeoloji, Epigrafive Tarihî Coḡrafyasi İçin Bibliyografya (1948), L'Année Philologique, Numismatic Literature, and Catalogue de la bibliothèque de l'école biblique de Jérusalem (1984) vol. 4. Moreover, each issue of the following journals and series (1895 forward) was searched for relevant archaeological reports and articles: American Journal of Archaeology; Anatolia (Anadolu); Anatolian Studies; Anzeiger der Österreichischen Akademie der Wissenschaften; Jahreshefte des Österreichischen Archäologischen Institutes (Hauptblatt; Beiblatt; Grabungen; Beiheft); Journal of Hellenic Studies (and Archaeology Reports); Türk Arkeoloji Dergisi; and Zeitschrift für die Papyrologie und Epigraphik.

In order to compile a bibliography of this type one must cast a net far and wide in the sea of available journals. At least half a dozen modern foreign languages and scores of journals are represented here. To exacerbate the bibliographer's task, there was no stylistic consistency among the authors and various bibliographic tools regarding the citation of various works. The most egregious examples of bibliographic antinomianism are to be found in European publications and dissertations. Clearly, "everyone did what was right in his own eyes." Consequently, I have made every effort to standardize as well as to verify personally each entry in the bibliography and to check for first names, correct spelling, pagination, and other bibliographical data. This necessary, albeit pedantic and laborious, routine would have been impossible without the cooperation of several libraries. Most notable among the libraries used were those at the Austrian Archaeological Institute, Harding University Graduate School of Religion, and Princeton University. Other libraries frequently used include those of Memphis State University, Rhodes College, Deutsches Archäologisches Institut (W. Berlin), University of Cincinnati, Vanderbilt University, and the University of Texas. The library staff of Harding University Graduate School of Religion, especially Mrs. Bonnie Baker, and Frau Maria Bodzenta at the Austrian Archaeological Institute were exceedingly helpful throughout months and months of questions and requests. Constant access to the library of the Austrian Archaeological Institute, the University of Vienna main library and numerous institute and seminar libraries at the University of Vienna was possible because of the kind assistance of Prof. Dr. Hermann Vetters, Director of the Austrian Archaeological Institute.

The tedium of typing and proofreading such a manuscript has fallen upon more than one innocent victim. Mrs. Jane Tomlinson and Mrs. Vee Brasfield typed on this during its embryonic stage. Mrs. Pam Shelby and Mrs. Catherine Wilcoxson typed on it during its later stages. Mrs. Jean Saunders receives my special thanks for the hours she spent typing as well as making bibliographic note cards in the early stage of the bibliography.

ABBREVIATIONS

1. AJA   American Journal of Archaeology

2. Anz. Wien   Anzeiger der phil.-hist. Klasse der Österreichischen Akademie der Wissenschaften

3. Hellenica   Hellenica, recueil d'épigraphie, de
                  numismatique et d'antiquités grecques

4. JÖAI   Jahreshefte des Österreichischen
                  Archäologischen Institutes

5. REG Bull. Epig. Revue des études grecques. Bulletin
                    épigraphique

6. ZPE   Zeitschrift für Papyrologie und
                  Epigraphik

    I will apologize in advance to anyone whose works I
perchance neglected; it was unintentional. I would hope to
hear from anyone with addenda et corrigenda for this bibliography.

Richard E. Oster
Harding University Graduate
School of Religion
1000 Cherry Road
Memphis, Tennessee 38117
Spring, 1986

INTRODUCTION

Bibliographies have at least one thing in common with dictionaries, namely, that while the best one is always less than perfect, even the worst is always better than none at all. A word about the origin and purview of this bibliographic effort is appropriate so that the user may know its strengths and weaknesses.

The origin of this bibliography can be traced to the author's long held, and continually increasing, conviction that the material culture and history of the sprawling urban center of imperial Ephesus have been too long ignored or inadequately treated by historians, exegetes, and archaeologists of primitive Christianity. Far too much evidence from Ephesus is extant and far too much of the literature of the first Christian century was written to or from Ephesus to overlook any longer the obvious correlation between the two. Several research trips during the past decade to the site of Ephesus and to the half dozen museums containing its principal off-site artifacts have significantly fortified this conviction. It was my good fortune that the American Theological Library Association came to share my conviction and awarded a grant that expedited the compilation and typing of a significant portion of this bibliography. This grant supplied the initial momentum that kept this tedious, and at times onerous, undertaking alive.

The scope of this bibliography is the ancient history, culture, and archaeological evidence of Ephesus. Though compiled to ameliorate the present situation of negligence and academic malpractice among many New Testament scholars, this bibliography will also be valuable to the ancient historian and archaeologist since many of the entries were authored by scholars in these disciplines.

Works written by New Testament and patristic scholars who have attempted to correlate their own disciplines with the history and culture of imperial Ephesus are also included. Since the archaic, classical, and Byzantine eras of history are not normally understood to fall within the scope of "New Testament History," only important representative works from these periods have been included in this bibliography. This circumscription is not, however, as limiting as it might first appear, since the great majority of artifacts and extant historical data concerning Ephesus stems, in fact, from the Roman period. Not listed here are works whose sole interest is the exegetical or doctrinal components of Ephesian Christianity, though scholarly research of an exegetical or theological nature would benefit greatly from a responsible appropriation of many of the titles in this bibliography.

THE EXCAVATIONS

It seems appropriate to introduce this bibliographic work with a precis of the history of the excavations of Ephesus. Those who have had the good fortune to visit the site of Ephesus in recent years know both the impressiveness of the ruins and the appreciation owed to the skillful archaeologists who have made this so.

As far back as the fifteenth century autobiographical records of European travelers and dilettantes narrate the story of those who sought to locate the temple of the Ephesian Artemis and to visit the seven churches of the Apocalypse. The narratives and travelogues of these early pilgrims typically contained laments about the paucity of extant ruins and monuments. Edmund Chishull provides an example of this from the eighteenth century. He complained that "the face of the whole (site) yields a melancholy and disagreeable prospect, being overrun with an incredible quantity of rank and luxuriant weeds, which serve only to corrupt the air, and conceal the curiosities of the place" (Antiquitates Asiaticae Christianam Aeram Antecedents, 1728).

This early period did, nevertheless, produce scholarly works and informative diaries, though written without the benefit of scientifically excavated artifacts. The best representatives of this era include Ernst Guhl, Ephesiaca (1843);

Charles Fellows, A Journal Written During an Excursion in
Asia Minor (1839); Edward Falkener, Ephesus and the Temple of Diana (1862); Francis Arundell, A Visit to the Seven
Churches of Asia (1828); and John Y. Akerman, Remarks on
the Coins of Ephesus Struck during the Roman Dominion
(1841). These authors worked with literary resources, visual surveys of the land, and to a lesser extent with coins
and epigraphical fragments found above ground. Most of
the significant architectural monuments were still hidden
from view.

The second era of Ephesus research was inaugurated
by the untiring efforts of John Turtle Wood. From 1863 to
1874 he was employed by the British Museum to, in his
words, "find the remains of the Great Temple of Diana which
had been buried for so many centuries." Remembering that
the science of archaeology was yet unborn (Heinrich Schlie-
mann had not yet made his epoch-making discoveries at Troy),
it comes as little surprise that Wood had been trained as an
architect. Moreover, he had to pay for the initial costs of
this expedition, though he was later supported by the British Museum.

His eleven-year project in Turkey yielded the desired
fruit. Not only did he discover the temple of the Ephesian
Artemis (on New Year's Eve, 1869), but he also excavated
large portions of the temple precinct, the Odeum and Great
Theatre, and unearthed numerous inscriptions, artifacts,
and coins. His success in such inhospitable circumstances
is an even greater tribute to his tenacity. Plagued by gangs
of robbers, malcontent workers, fortune hunters, malaria,
unharvested barley fields, and inclement weather, he continued his work from season to season. He and Mrs. Wood
left only when funds were terminated by the British Museum.
Some years later (1904-1905) the British Museum briefly supported further excavation of the site of the Artemis temple
under the direction of David Hogarth.

The third major period of discovery and research began
in the late nineteenth century. In 1895 the Austrian Archaeological Institute in Vienna began systematic excavations at
Ephesus under the direction of Otto Benndorf. The Institute
still has the principal responsibility for the ongoing excavations and restorations there. It is due to the assiduous efforts of the Austrian Archaeological Institute, which have

abated only in times of military and diplomatic turmoil (prin-
cipally during the periods 1914-1925 and 1936-1953), that
Ephesus is one of the best excavated and restored Anatolian
cities from the Graeco-Roman era. Moreover, it has been
during this third period that most of the significant publications as well as most of the systematic interpretation of
the discoveries has taken place.

INSCRIPTIONS

During a brief spring sojourn in Ephesus in 1699, a
certain Edmund Chishull noted the following:

> It is to be wished, that some curious traveler might
> remain two or three days at Ephesus; during which
> time by removing the weeds, and clearing the con-
> fused ruins, he might possibly discover many valu-
> able inscriptions [p. 28].

Needless to say, the corpus of Ephesian epigraphy far
exceeds two or three days' work worth of valuable inscriptions. This site has yielded more than 4,000 Greek and
Latin inscriptions. Virtually every year new inscriptions
come to light. The base of a small votive monument, pillars
of municipal buildings, public latrine walls, and commemora-
tive stone plaques all make epigraphic contributions to our
knowledge of ancient Ephesus.

The information recorded in this epigraphy is highly
significant. One of the earliest discovered inscriptions
(Salutaris inscription) provided the needed information for
discovering the foundation of the Artemis temple, long buried underground. It did this by narrating the urban route
of the sacred processional from the temple of Artemis to the
city theater and back again, through a different city gate,
to the temple of Artemis. By following this path Wood was
eventually led to the long lost site of the Artemis temple.
This stone record, along with others, has furnished important, and sometimes unique, information concerning the beliefs, festivals, and rites of the devotees of the Ephesian
Artemis.

The data afforded in these inscriptions become increas-
ingly significant in the study of other religious cults and

beliefs in Ephesus. Names of individual priests of the gods Dionysus, Apollo, and Asclepius are preserved. The importance of the Egyptian deities in Ephesus comes to the foreground when one realizes that they are mentioned in epigraphical remains which span over a five-hundred-year period. Furthermore, it is only from epigraphical evidence that one learns that the cult of Alexander the Great was still maintained in Ephesus in the imperial era.

The use of various Greek words and phrases in the Ephesian inscriptions should be of interest to the student of the primitive church. The use of the Greek verb apostello, for example, to describe the action of religious and cultic officials of the Artemis religion is noteworthy. Investigation of the numerous epigraphical references to the silversmiths' guild (argyrokopos) will shed light upon the narrative of Acts 19:22-40. Another inscription, discovered over a century ago, mentions deacons and deaconesses of a cult of Zeus, one of whose cultic duties was associated with religious water immersions (hydrobaphos). These three examples of the Greek terms apostello, argyrokopos, and hydrobaphos are merely a small sample from a large corpus of epigraphical data yet to be explored by New Testament scholars.

NUMISMATICS

The ancient coinage of Ephesus has provided numismatists with a pictorial and iconographic perspective on the city and its life. Numerous cults, both local and foreign, are attested by Ephesian coins. These include Apollo, Ephesian Artemis, Egyptian deities, Hekate, Hercules, Isis, Dionysus, Zeus, and local river gods, to name only a few. Memory of various historic occasions as well as culturally significant individuals is likewise preserved on coins. Ephesian mintage also contains valuable records of Roman emperors and the development of the imperial cult in the Greek East. Furthermore, these coins provided not only a visual medium for creating as well as maintaining the metropolitan ethos of imperial Ephesus, but also supplied a medium for preserving pictures of ancient monuments and temples that have since been destroyed.

Mythic symbolism is also prominent on these coins.

For example, the hieros gamos concept, which has been so
dominant in the exegesis and interpretation of Ephesians
chapter 5, is emblematized on an Ephesian coin dating from
the Julio-Claudian era. The religious use of astral power
language, numerology, and theriomorphic epiphanies that
often found currency on Ephesian mintage of the imperial
period provides provocative landscape for the interpretation
of the symbolism of the Apocalypse of John. Finally, the
primeval account of the victory of good over evil, symbo-
lized by the defeat of the dragon serpent, was at home not
only in early Christian writings (e.g. Rev. 12:1-17; cf.
Rom. 16:20) but also in the iconography used at Ephesus
during the Greek as well as Roman periods of history.

ARCHITECTURAL MONUMENTS, PLASTIC ARTS, PAINTINGS, ETC.

Mosaics, frescoes, statues, restored buildings and
monuments are the most impressive visual fruit of the archaeologist's work. Excavated agorae, numerous homes
with their wall paintings, statues, and mosaics, and public
fountains and buildings illuminate the commercial, domestic,
religious, and civic side of ancient urban life. The mere
artistic style of extant Ephesian statuary can be an important indicator of certain cultural trends of the city. Moreover, one cannot prepare a very accurate reconstruction of
the significance of urban philosophy, rhetoric, and education in Ephesus (and the network which connected them)
without first working through the relevant material culture
extant in frescoes, sarcophagi, mosaics, and the plastic
arts.

In the area of architecture, the twenty-five-thousand-
seat theater at Ephesus must be understood as much more
than a visually dominant structure in Roman Ephesus used
for staging drama and comedy. It also played a role, often
a key role, in the political, religious, and civic life of metropolitan Ephesus. Several temples have been excavated
there, including those of foreign, indigenous, and imperial
cults. Equally important at Ephesus was the discovery of a
private religious chapel, solely for cultic and communal activities, constructed in an individual's home.

NEGLECT OF EPHESUS IN RECENT
NEW TESTAMENT SCHOLARSHIP

The past few decades have seen the rebirth of a fresh interest in studying the milieu of early Christianity from various historical, sociological, and anthropological perspectives. Such catchwords as social history, social description, communities, ethos, symbolic, millenarian cults, paradigm-shifts, and networks now appear frequently in the scholarly literature. The use of photographs (unfortunately often presented with neither coherent relationship to the text of the book nor with a discernible interpretive significance) to depict ancient landscapes or artifacts also reflects this increasing commitment to investigate more responsibly the milieu of earliest Christianity. Accordingly, Rudolf Bultmann's truncated method and focus on the "history of self understanding" is now moribund, and rightly so.

This renaissance of the historical-sociological approach can only be celebrated. Notwithstanding the appropriate kudos, it must be remembered that birth is followed by infancy, and infancy by immaturity. Immaturity in the selection and use of ancient archaeological sources is still the state-of-the-art in many academic quarters as New Testament scholarship is just learning to walk among the vast number of archaeological facts in front of it.

There is no clearer example of the neglect of potentially relevant historical and archaeological sources than at Ephesus. While the charge of neglecting Ephesus could be brought against numerous dissertations and journal articles published in the past two decades, it seems better to highlight three particular books published in the last decade.

I have chosen to note briefly certain problems in the works of professors John Gager, Helmut Koester, and Wayne Meeks. The choice of these scholars was made for two reasons: 1) the cynosural role each of them serves in American scholarship and 2) the fact that each of their works reflects significantly discrete methods as well as conclusions.

Professor John G. Gager's book Kingdom and Community. The Social World of Early Christianity (1975) was written with a penchant for correlating elements within primitive

Christianity to the rubrics provided by "more exotic religions" as well as by psychoanalysis and sociology. Gager
clearly eschews the approaches and methodologies of the
typical social historian who wishes to reconstruct and correlate the social institutions of the ancient world with those
of the early church. Following the sociological perspectives
of Berger, Burridge, and others, he seeks to explore the
social dimensions within Christian communities themselves.
Gager was apparently unaware that a prominent archaeologist at Ephesus (Dr. Anton Bammer) with similar interests
in the categories of sociology, psychoanalysis, and struc-
turalism has written extensively on Ephesus. Moreover,
Gager's proclivity for theory rather than data has led to
superficialities in his efforts to analyze particular facets of
early Christianity. As the author himself acknowledges, the
character of his studies is "experimental, almost gamelike"
(p. xii).

The following two examples were missed opportunities
for the possible correlation between Gager's studies and
Ephesian culture. In the first instance, the "Attainment of
Millennial Bliss through Myth: The Book of Revelation"
(pp. 49-65) reflects a truncated data base for investigation.
In this chapter Gager ignores the existence and manipulation
of dualistic symbols and myths in the ancient Ephesian community. On another point, Professor Gager observes that
"various elements of early Christian ethics can best be understood as efforts to capture in the present the conditions
of the future ... the abolition at least in theory, of premil-
lennial distinctions between male and female, Jew and Greek,
slave and free ... " (p. 50). Is it not at least worthy of
mention that the major civil religion of Ephesus strove to
address the human categories of "Greek and barbarian" and
"slave and free" through means of its theology and cultic
activities?

Gager is not alone in failing to consider the culture
and symbols of ancient Ephesus. Helmut Koester also neg-
lects the available artifacts of imperial Ephesus, though it
should be noted that his work is different in scope and
methodology from Gager's and reflects greater erudition and
comprehensiveness. This failure is ironic since he has so
eloquently defended the necessity of studying primitive
Christianity in regional as well as temporal units. He argued earlier (James Robinson and Helmut Koester, Trajectories through Early Christianity, pp. 276-77),

We have learned to distinguish between the different periods of Christian history in the first centuries. We are also beginning to realize that phenomena from the religion of the Hellenistic and Roman eras must be dated with some precision before they can be utilized to determine the interrelationships within Christian, Jewish and pagan religions. It is equally necessary to focus on the particular situation in a limited geographical area in order to understand the interplay between Christianity and culture in antiquity. Trajectories must be plotted in grids that reflect shifts in space as well as in time.

Unfortunately, Koester's Einführung in das Neue Testament im Rahmen der Religionsgeschichte und Kulturgeschichte der hellenistischen und römischen Zeit (1980) falls short of his own stated standards. In responding to rather specific criticism [Eckhard Plümacher, Göttingische Gelehrte Anzeigen 233 (1981):1-23] he included a cursory chapter in the English translation (Introduction to the New Testament. History, Culture, and Religion of the Hellenistic Age, 1982) of his work entitled, "The Cities in the Roman Empire" (I:332-36). Lamentably, he still shows little awareness of the material culture and imperial history of Ephesus, even though he himself stresses that it was the urban location for the majority of Paul's literary activity (II:116).

Koester's failure to note parallels between primitive Christian experiences and trajectories and their specific urban context at Ephesus stands in sharp contrast with his expressed conviction that

> The conquests of Alexander the Great led to the formation of a new political and economic order of large dimensions.... Christianity developed as part of the culture of this new world, one in which important processes of cultural and religious interpretation and amalgamation had taken place during the Hellenistic period.... It is exactly these major Hellenistic cities in which early Christianity was formed and developed its potential as a new world religion [I:XXXIII-XXXIV].

In the recent book entitled The First Urban Christians. The Social World of the Apostle Paul (1983), Wayne Meeks is likewise remiss in treating the history and culture of imperial

Ephesus. Though Meeks acknowledges that the city of Ephesus played an important role in the life and ministry of the apostle Paul, he avoids Ephesus in deference to Corinth and Thessalonica. His reason for such neglect is not explicitly stated, but may be implicit in a specious statement about Ephesus when he writes that "like most of the monuments that immediately impress the visitor to the excavated site today, it [temple of Sarapis] was built at a period later than the one that interests us" (p. 44). First of all, there are several important monuments and structures at Ephesus that do date from the period that interests Meeks. Second, there is a plethora of artifacts--coins, inscriptions, statues, and frescoes--that are very germaine for reconstructing the urban ethos contemporary with Pauline Christianity. Several topics of interest in Meeks's analysis of urban Christianity could have been correlated with this extant evidence.

Finally, the fact that a monument like the temple of Sarapis was built a century or more after Paul's tenure in Ephesus does not a priori relegate it to the trash heap of irrelevance for studying the Ephesus of Paul's day, especially in light of the fact that Egyptian cults had constantly played an important role in Ephesus' religious life for centuries before the advent of Paul.

One is puzzled by the neglect of ancient Ephesus in current New Testament scholarship. The genesis of the problem cannot be attributed to a dearth of New Testament documents stemming from primitive Christianity in Ephesus. Notwithstanding one's views of the authorship of various letters in the Pauline corpus or of the accuracy of Luke's picture in Acts 19-20, the city of Ephesus is too deeply imbedded in the various sources and traditions of the early church to sweep it under the rug with the broom of authorship questions. Thus, the question of the authorship of the Pastoral Letters or of Ephesians is not inextricably tied to either the question of their destination or their provenance. In an analogous case, Professor Karl Donfried has recently argued that the material culture and history of ancient Thessalonica is relevant for interpreting II Thessalonians, regardless of Pauline authorship ("The Cults of Thessalonica and the Thessalonian Correspondence." New Testament Studies 31 [1985]:336-56).

In addition, one cannot justify this neglect with the

suggestion that the excavations at Ephesus have not pro-
duced significant artifacts generally contemporary with earliest Christianity. Falling within the chronological boundaries
of the Graeco-Roman civilization normally assumed in the
study of the literature, history, and development of primitive Christianity, there are, in addition to the ancient literature, thousands of inscriptions, coins, statues and monuments that illumine the historical landscape of primitive
Christianity in Ephesus.

There are several plausible explanations for this neglect. If there is a confluence of contributing factors, I
would suggest the following tentative list:

1. Acute ignorance of the availability and significance
   of Ephesian data in the reconstruction and correlation of the Ephesian milieu of primitive Christianity.

2. Residual influence from a previous generation of
   scholarship which was philosophically and theolog-
   ically suspicious of, and at times hostile to, the
   correlation of historical and cultural phenomena
   with the kerygma or supposed kernel of early
   Christian faith.

3. Crippling dependence on the secondary works of
   other scholars, often classicists such as A. D.
   Nock, E. R. Dodds, Ramsay MacMullen, who themselves have, at times, been less than infallible.

4. The "Holy Land captivity" of archaeology in North
   American seminaries, universities, and journals of
   Bible archaeology.

5. Rationalizing defense mechanisms; for example,
   "one's own mortality" or "There aren't enough
   hours in the day."

6. The inability to distinguish between a quasi-
   pilgrimage to photograph sites and rigorous research, resulting in a failure to correlate artifacts and culture.

7. The relative inaccessibility to New Testament scholars of training, field experience, adequate libraries,

and formal instruction in classical epigraphy,
numismatics, art history and iconography, and
archaeology.

Admittedly, the following bibliography is no panacea
for all of the above-mentioned ills. If used to its fullest,
however, it will serve as a catalyst for fresh research, the
fruits of which in turn could help to mature New Testament
exegesis, theology, and especially the subdiscipline known
as the social description of primitive Christianity.

THE BIBLIOGRAPHY

1 Abbott, Frank F., and Johnson, Allan C. Municipal Administration in the Roman Empire. Princeton: Princeton University Press, 1926.

2 Abramić, Michael. "Antike Kopien griechischer Skulpturen in Dalmatien." In Festschrift für Rudolf Egger. Beiträge zur älteren Europäischen Kulturgeschichte. Klagenfurt: Verlag des Geschichtsvereins für Kärnten, 1953, 1:303-26.

3 Adams, John P. "Aristonikos and Cistophoroi." Historia 29 (1980):302-14.

4 Akerman, John Y. Remarks on the Coins of Ephesus Struck during the Roman Dominion. London: J. Wertheimer & Co., 1841.

5 _____. "Remarks on the Coins of Ephesus Struck during the Roman Dominion." Numismatic Chronicle 4 (1842):73-118.

6 Akşit, Ilhan. "Ephesos." In The Civilization of Western Anatolia. Istanbul: Akşit Culture and Tourism Publications, 1985, pp. 26-55.

7 Akurgal, Ekrem. Ancient Civilizations and Ruins of Turkey from Prehistoric Times until the End of the Roman Empire. 1st ed. Istanbul: Mobil Oil Türk, 1969, pp. 142-71.

8 _____. Ancient Civilizations and Ruins of Turkey from Prehistoric Times until the End of the Roman Empire. 2nd ed. Istanbul: Mobil Oil Türk, 1970, pp. 142-71.

9 _____. Ancient Civilizations and Ruins of Turkey

from Prehistoric Times until the End of the Roman Empire. 3rd ed. Ankara: Türk Tarih Kurumu Basimevi, 1973, pp. 142-70.

10 _____. Ancient Civilizations and Ruins of Turkey from Prehistoric Times until the End of the Roman Empire. 4th ed. Ankara: Türk Tarih Kurumu Basimevi, 1978, pp. 142-71, 378-84.

11 _____. Ancient Civilizations and Ruins of Turkey from Prehistoric Times until the End of the Roman Empire. 5th ed. Ankara: Türk Tarih Kurumu Basimevi, 1983.

12 _____. Ancient Civilizations and Ruins of Turkey from Prehistoric Times until the End of the Roman Empire. 6th ed. Ankara: Türk Tarih Kurumu Basimevi, 1985, pp. 142-71, 378-84.

13 _____. "Eine ephesische Elfenbeinstatuette aus Erythrai." In Lebendige Altertumswissenschaft. Festgabe zur Vollendung des 70. Lebensjahres von Hermann Vetters dargebracht von Freunden, Schülern und Kollegen. Vienna: Verlag Adolf Holzhausens Nfg., 1985, pp. 43-49.

14 _____. "Hitit sanatinin Yunan sanatina tesirleri." IV. Türk Tarih Kongresi. Ankara: Türk Tarih Kurumu Basimevi, 1952, pp. 45-51.

15 Alföldi, András. "Iuba 1. und die Pompeianer in Africa (zu den Münzquellen der Geschichte der Bürgerkriege, I)." Gazette Numismatique Suisse 8 (1958):103-08; 9 (1959):1-5.

16 Alföldi, Elisabeth; Erim, Kenan; and Inan, Jale. "Roman and early Byzantine Portrait Sculpture in Asia Minor." Belleten 32 (1968):1-24.

Alföldi-Rosenbaum, Elisabeth. See no. 595.

17 Alföldy, Géza, and Halfmann, Helmut. "Iunius Maximus und die Victoria Parthica." ZPE 35 (1979):195-212.

18 Alkim, Handan. "Explorations and Excavations in Turkey, 1965 and 1966." Anatolica 2 (1968):1-76.

19 Almgren, Bertil. "Basilikan vid Kustur och havsytans förändringar." Svenska Forskningsinstitutet i Istanbul. Meddelanden 1 (1976):58-61.

20 Alzinger, Wilhelm. "Alt-Ephesos, Topographie und Architektur." Das Altertum 13 (1967):20-44.

21 _____. "Die Altertümer von Belevi. Versuch einer topographischen, archäologischen und historischen Einordnung." In Forschungen in Ephesos, vol. 6: Das Mausoleum von Belevi. Vienna: Österreichisches Archäologisches Institut, 1979, pp. 167-200.

22 _____. "Die Arbeiten des österreichischen archäologischen Institutes im Frühjahr: 1972." Efes Harabeleri ve Müzesi Yilliği 1 (1972):43-45.

23 _____. "Aspectus pronai aedis Augusti." In Akten des Vitruv-Kolloquiums, Darmstadt, 1982. (Darmstadt: Wissenschaftliche Buchgesellschaft, 1982, pp. 185-91.

24 _____. "Athen und Ephesos in fünften Jahrhundert von Christus." In The Proceedings of the Xth International Congress of Classical Archaeology. Edited by E. Akurgal. Ankara: Türk Tarih Kurumu Basimevi, 1978, 1:507-16.

25 _____. "Augusteische Architektur in Ephesos." In Roman Frontier Studies 1967. The Proceedings of the 7th International Congress Held at Tel Aviv. Tel Aviv: University Press, 1971, pp. 132-41.

26 _____. Augusteische Architektur in Ephesos. Sonderschrift, 16. Vienna: Österreichisches Archäologisches Institut, 1974.

27 _____. "Bildmessung und Archäologie." JÖAI 48 (1966-1967):Grabungen in 1967, 47-51.

28 _____. "Disiecta membra." JÖAI 50 (1972-1975): Beibl. 87-94.

29 _____. "Ephesiaca." JÖAI 56 (1985):59-64.

30 _____. "Ephesos: B. Archäologischer Teil." In

Paulys Realencyclopädie der classischen Altertumswissenschaft. Supplementband. Edited by K. Ziegler. Stuttgart: Alfred Druckenmüller Verlag, 1970, 12:1588-1704 (Nachträge).

31 _____. "Frühformen der römischen Marktbasilika." Römische Historische Mitteilungen 26 (1984):31-41.

32 _____. "Ionische Kapitelle aus Ephesos I." JÖAI 46 (1961-1963):105-36.

33 _____. "Ionische Kapitelle aus Ephesos I (Nachtrag zu ÖJh 46, 1961-63 Hauptblatt S. 121ff. Nr. 5)." JÖAI 46 (1961-1963):Beibl. 31-34.

34 _____. "Koressos." In Festschrift für Fritz Eichler zum achtzigsten Geburtstag. Vienna: Österreichisches Archäologisches Institut, 1967, pp. 1-9.

35 _____. "Das Regierungsviertel." JÖAI 50 (1972-1975):Grabungen in Ephesos von 1960-1969 bzw. 1970, 229-300.

36 _____. "Ritzzeichnungen in den Marmorbrüchen von Ephesos." JÖAI 48 (1966-1967):61-72.

37 _____. Die Ruinen von Ephesos. Vienna: A. F. Koska, 1972.

38 _____. Die Stadt des siebenten Weltwunders. Die Wiederentdeckung von Ephesos. Vienna: Morawa & Co., 1962.

39 _____. "Von der Archaik zur Klassik. Zur Entwicklung des ionischen Kapitells in Kleinasien während des fünften Jahrhunderts v. Chr." JÖAI 50 (1972-1975):169-211.

40 _____. "Wandernde Künstler und ionische Spiralen in früharchaischer Zeit." In Classica et Provincialia. Festschrift für Erna Diez. Edited by G. Schwarz and E. Pochmarski. Graz: Akademische Druck und Verlagsanstalt, 1978, pp. 17-32.

41 _____. "Zwei spätantike Porträtköpfe aus Ephesos." JÖAI 42 (1955):27-42.

_____. See nos. 764, 1241.

42 Alzinger, Wilhelm, and Bammer, Anton. Forschungen in
    Ephesos. Vol. 7: Das Monument des C. Memmius.
    Vienna: Österreichisches Archäologisches Institut,
    1971.

43 Alzinger, Wilhelm, and Hueber, Friedmund. Ephesos.
    Lebendige Vergangenheit. Giessen: Mikado-Verlag,
    1972.

44 Alzinger, Wilhelm, and Knibbe, Dieter. Ephesos. Ein
    Rundgang durch die Ruinen. Vienna: A. F. Koska,
    1972.

45 Amelung, Walther. "Zwei ephesische Fragmente." JÖAI
    12 (1909):172-82.

46 Ampolo, C. "L'Artemide di Marsiglia e la Diana dell'
    Aventino." Parola del passato 25 (1970):200-210.

47 Andreae, Bernard. Odysseus. Archäologie des euro-
    päischen Menschenbildes. Frankfurt: Societäts-
    Verlag, 1982. pp. 69-90.

48 _____. "Die Polyphem-Gruppe von Ephesos." In
    Lebendige Altertumswissenschaft. Festgabe zur
    Vollendung des 70. Lebensjahres von Hermann
    Vetters dargebracht von Freunden, Schülern und
    Kollegen. Vienna: Verlag Adolf Holzhausens Nfg.,
    1985, pp. 209-211.

49 _____. "Vorschlag für eine Rekonstruktion der Poly-
    phemgruppe von Ephesos." In Festschrift für Frank
    Brommer. Edited by U. von Hoeckmann and A. Krug.
    Mainz: Verlag Philipp von Zabern, 1977, pp. 1-11.

50 Antoine, P. "Ephèse." In Dictionnaire de la Bible,
    Supplément. Edited by L. Pirot. Paris: Letouzey
    et Ané, 1934, 2:1076-1104.

51 Armbruster, Ludwig. "Die Biene in der Kunst." Archiv
    für Bienenkunde; Zeitschrift für Bienenwissen und
    Bienenwirtschaft 18 (1937):49-86.

52 Arnold, Irene R. "Festivals of Ephesus." AJA 76 (1972):17-22.

53 Arsan, Nimet. "Anadolu'nun M.S.I. ve II. yüzyillarina ait giyimli ve ayakta duran kadin heykelleri." Belleten 10 (1946):425-70.

54 Arundell, Francis V. J. A Visit to the Seven Churches of Asia; with an Excursion into Pisidia; Containing Remarks on the Geography and Antiquities of Those Countries, a Map of the Author's Routes and Numerous Inscriptions. London: John Rodwell, 1828.

55 Asheri, David. "Leggi greche sul problema dei debiti." Studi Classici e Orientali 18 (1969):5-122.

56 Atalay, Erol. "Die antiken Mamorsteinbrüche von Kusini." In Lebendige Altertumswissenschaft. Festgabe zur Vollendung des 70. Lebensjahres von Hermann Vetters dargebracht von Freunden, Schülern und Kollegen. Vienna: Verlag Adolf Holzhausens Nfg., 1985, pp. 311-14.

57 _____. "Antiker Marmorsteinbruch bei Ephesos." JÖAI 51 (1976-1977):59-60.

58 _____. "Ein archaisches Frauenkopffragment aus dem Artemision." Efes Müzesi Yilliği 2 (1973-1978):33-37.

59 _____. "Eine christliche Kulthöhle aus Ephesos," JÖAI 54 (1983):129-31.

60 _____. "Efes (Selçuk) Müzesinde Bulunan Karikatür Terracottalar." Ege Üniversitesi Edebiyat Fakültesi Arkeoloji ve Sanat Tarihi Dergisi 11 (1983):5.

61 _____. "Efes'de Büyük Tiyatro'nun restorasyonu için yapilan kazilar ve bu kazilardan elde edilen buluntular." Efes Harabeleri ve Müzesi Yilliği 1 (1972): 49-55.

62 _____. "Efes'te Bulunan Hellenistik porte (Önrapor)." Türk Arkeoloji Dergisi 19.1 (1970):213-15.

63 _____. "Ephesos çevresindeki magaralarin arkeoloji

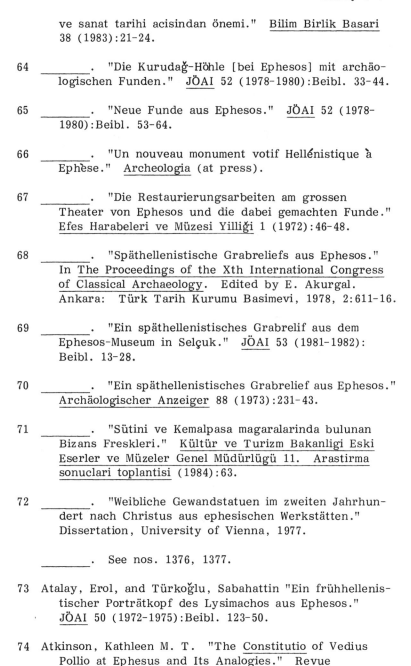

ve sanat tarihi acisindan önemi." Bilim Birlik Basari
38 (1983):21-24.

64 _____. "Die Kurudağ-Höhle [bei Ephesos] mit archäologischen Funden." JÖAI 52 (1978-1980):Beibl. 33-44.

65 _____. "Neue Funde aus Ephesos." JÖAI 52 (1978-
1980):Beibl. 53-64.

66 _____. "Un nouveau monument votif Hellénistique à
Ephèse." Archeologia (at press).

67 _____. "Die Restaurierungsarbeiten am grossen
Theater von Ephesos und die dabei gemachten Funde."
Efes Harabeleri ve Müzesi Yilliği 1 (1972):46-48.

68 _____. "Späthellenistische Grabreliefs aus Ephesos."
In The Proceedings of the Xth International Congress
of Classical Archaeology. Edited by E. Akurgal.
Ankara: Türk Tarih Kurumu Basimevi, 1978, 2:611-16.

69 _____. "Ein späthellenistisches Grabrelif aus dem
Ephesos-Museum in Selçuk." JÖAI 53 (1981-1982):
Beibl. 13-28.

70 _____. "Ein späthellenistisches Grabrelief aus Ephesos."
Archäologischer Anzeiger 88 (1973):231-43.

71 _____. "Sütini ve Kemalpasa magaralarinda bulunan
Bizans Freskleri." Kültür ve Turizm Bakanligi Eski
Eserler ve Müzeler Genel Müdürlügü 11. Arastirma
sonuclari toplantisi (1984):63.

72 _____. "Weibliche Gewandstatuen im zweiten Jahrhundert nach Christus aus ephesischen Werkstätten."
Dissertation, University of Vienna, 1977.

_____. See nos. 1376, 1377.

73 Atalay, Erol, and Türkoğlu, Sabahattin "Ein frühhellenis-
tischer Porträtkopf des Lysimachos aus Ephesos."
JÖAI 50 (1972-1975):Beibl. 123-50.

74 Atkinson, Kathleen M. T. "The Constitutio of Vedius
Pollio at Ephesus and Its Analogies." Revue

internationale des droits de l'antiquité 3rd ser. 9
(1962):261-89.

75 Aufhauser, J. B. "Wo befindet sich das echte
Mariengrab, in Jerusalem oder bei Ephesus?" In
Akten 24. Internationales Orientalisten Kongresses.
Wiesbaden: Franz Steiner Verlag, 1959, pp. 230-33.

76 Aulock, Hans S. von. "Kleinasiatische Münzstätten."
Jahrbuch für Numismatik und Geldgeschichte 19
(1969):79-88.

77 _____. Sammlung von Aulock. vol. 6 Ionien. Sylloge
nummorum Graecorum. Deutschland. Berlin: Gebr.
Mann, 1957-1968.

77a Aurenhammer, Maria. "Arbeitsbericht Ephesos 1983."
Anz. Wien 121 (1984):216-18.

78 _____. "Athena Medici in Ephesos." In Lebendige
Altertumswissenschaft. Festgabe zur Vollendung des
70. Lebensjahres von Hermann Vetters dargebracht
von Freunden, Schülern und Kollegen. Vienna:
Verlag Adolf Holzhausens Nfg., 1985, pp. 212-15.

79 _____. "Römische Porträts aus Ephesos. Neue Funde
aus dem Hanghaus 2." JÖAI 54 (1983):Beibl. 105-46.

80 Aygel, Cemal. Efesos Tarihi ve Harabeleri. Izmir:
Teknik Kitap ve Mecmua, 1959.

81 Aziz, A. [= A. Aziz Ogan]. Efesus-Ayaslug Rehberi.
Izmir, 1927.

82 _____. Guide du Musée de Smyrne. Istanbul:
Resimli Ay Matbaasi Ltd., 1933.

83 _____. Izmir Müzesi Rehberi. Istanbul: Resimli Ay
Matbaasi Ltd. Sirketi, 1932.

84 _____. "1926 Senesi Efes Hafriyati." Maarif Vekaleti
Mecmuasi 10 (1928):40-57.

85 _____. "1927 Senesi Efes Hafriyati." Maarif Vekaleti
Mecumasi 15 (1928):475-91.

86 _____. "1928 Senesi Efes Hafriyati." Maarif Vekaleti
Mecumasi 17 (1929):101-19.

87 Babelon, Ernest. "Quatre médaillons de bronze d'Asie
Mineure." Revue numismatique 3rd ser. 9 (1891):
26-39.

88 Babelon, Jean. "Offrandes monétaires à des statues
culturelles." Revue numismatique 5th ser. 7 (1943):
1-9.

89 _____. "La pénétration romaine en Asie Mineure d'après
les documents numismatiques." Revue numismatique
5th ser. 3 (1939):1-42, 149-88.

90 Babinger, Franz. "Die Ortlichkeit der Siebenschläfer-
legende in muslimischer Schau." Anz. Wien 94
(1957):87-95.

91 Bakhuizen van den Brink, Jan Nicolaas. De Oud-
christelijke Monumenten van Ephesus: Epigraphische
Studie. Den Haag: De Nederlandsche Boek-en
Steendruklerij, 1923.

92 Balaban, Rahmi. Efes. Izmir: Dost Basimevi, 1946.

93 Bamm, Peter [Emmrich, Kurt]. Frühe Stätten der
Christenheit. Munich: Kösel-Verlag, 1955, pp. 124-
66.

94 Bammer, Anton. "Der Altar des jüngeren Artemisions
von Ephesos." Archäologischer Anzeiger 83 (1968):
400-423.

95 _____. "The Altar of Artemis at Ephesus." Efes
Harabeleri ve Müzesi Yilliği 1 (1972):76-82.

96 _____. "Amazonen und das Artemision von Ephesos."
Revue archéologique n.s. 1 (1976):91-102.

97 _____. "Der archaische und klassische Altar der
Artemis von Ephesos." In The Proceedings of the
Xth International Congress of Classical Archaeology.

Edited by E. Akurgal. Ankara: Türk Tarih Kurumu Basimevi, 1978, 1:517-21.

98 _____. "Architektur." JÖAI 50 (1972-1975): Grabungen in Ephesos von 1960-1979 bzw. 1970, 381-406.

99 _____. Die Architektur des jüngeren Artemision von Ephesos. Wiesbaden: Franz Steiner Verlag, 1972.

99a _____. Architektur und Gesellschaft in der Antike. 2nd. ed. Kulturstudien, 5. Vienna: Hermann Böhlaus, 1985.

100 _____. "Architektur und Gesellschaft in der Antike." In Architektur und Gesellschaft von der Antike bis zur Gegenwart. Edited by H. Stekl. Geschichte und Sozialkunde, 6. Salzburg: Verlag Wolfgang Neugebauer, 1980, pp. 15-70, 402-406.

101 _____. "Architektur und Klassizismus." Hephaistos 3 (1981):95-106.

102 _____. "Architecture et société en Asie Mineure au IVe siècle." In Architecture et société de l'archaïsme grec à la fin de la république romaine. Collection de l'Ecole française de Rome, 1980. Paris: Centre National de la Recherche Scientifique, 1983, pp. 271-300.

103 _____. "Beiträge zur ephesischen Architektur, I: Zum Eckkapitell eines Ringhallentempels; II: Ein Rundfries mit Bukranien und Girlanden: 23-40." JÖAI 49 (1968-1971):1-22.

104 _____. "Beobachtungen zur ephesischen Architektur." Archäologischer Anzeiger 87 (1972):440-57.

105 _____. "Chronologische und stratigraphische Probleme der archaischen Kultanlagen im Artemision von Ephesos." Hephaistos 5-6 (1983-1984):91ff.

106 _____. "Das Denkmal des C. Sextilius Pollio in Ephesos." JÖAI 51 (1976-1977):Beibl. 77-92.

107 _____. "Efes Artemis tapinaği sunağinda yapilan

çalişmalar." Efes Harabeleri ve Müzesi Yilliği 1 (1972):83.

108 _____. "Elemente flavisch-trajanischer Architekturfassaden aus Ephesos." JÖAI 52 (1978-1980):67-90.

109 _____. "Die Entwicklung des Opferkultes am Altar der Artemis von Ephesos." Istanbuler Mitteilungen 23-24 (1973-1974):53-62.

110 _____. "Forschungen im Artemision von Ephesos von 1976 bis 1981." Anatolian Studies 32 (1982):61-87.

111 _____. "Die gebrannten Mauerziegel von Ephesos und ihre Datierung." JÖAI 47 (1964-1965):Beibl. 289-300.

112 _____. "Geometrie und Ornament als Antithese bei Doppelmäandern in Ephesos." In Festschrift für Fritz Eichler zum achtzigsten Geburtstag. Vienna: Österreichisches Archäologisches Institut, 1967, pp. 10-22.

113 _____. Das Heiligtum der Artemis von Ephesos. Graz: Akademische Druck-u. Verlagsanstalt, 1984.

114 _____. "Hellenistische Kapitelle aus Ephesos." Mitteilungen des Deutschen Archäologischen Instituts (Athenische Abteilung) 88 (1973):219-34.

115 _____. "Neue Forschungen am Altar des Artemisions von Ephesos." Archäologischer Anzeiger 87 (1972): 714-28.

116 _____. "Neue Grabungen beim Artemision von Ephesos." Antike Kunst 13 (1970):114-15.

117 _____. "Neue weibliche Statuetten aus dem Artemision von Ephesos." JÖAI 56 (1985):39-58.

118 _____. "Die politische Symbolik des Memmiusbaues." JÖAI 50 (1972-1973):220-22.

119 _____. "Recent Excavations at the Altar of Artemis in Ephesus." Archaeology 27 (1974):202-5.

120 _____. "Ein spätantiker Torbau aus Ephesos."
JÖAI 51 (1976-1977):Beibl. 93-126.

121 _____. "Spuren der Phöniker im Artemision von
Ephesos." Anatolian Studies 35 (1985):103-108.

122 _____. "Tempel und Altar der Artemis von Ephesos."
JÖAI 48 (1966-1967):Beibl. 21-44.

123 _____. "Über die Grundlagen und Ergebnisse des
Paläomagnetismus und die Bestimmung der paläo-
magnetischen Inklination mit antiken Ziegeln von
Ephesos in Kleinasien." Dissertation, University of
Vienna, 1965.

124 _____. "Wo einst ein Weltwunder stand. Letzte
Ergebnisse österreichischer Forschungen im antiken
Ephesos." Das Altertum 21 (1975):27-35.

125 _____. "Zu den Kapitellen des Altars von Pergamon."
Forschungen und Berichte--Staatliche Museen Berlin
16 (1974):183-90.

126 _____. "Zu ÖJh 50, 1972-1975 Beibl. 242ff. 249ff."
JÖAI 51 (1976-1977):57-58.

127 _____. "Zum Durchmesser jonischer Säulen." JÖAI
49 (1968-71):Beibl. 89-92.

128 _____. "Zum jüngeren Artemision von Ephesos. Die
Terrasse des jüngeren Artemisions und eustathische
Schwankungen des Meeresspiegels." JÖAI 47 (1964-
1965):126-45.

129 _____. "Zur soziologischen Deutung ephesischer
Architektur." Istanbuler Mitteilungen 25 (1975):
319-34.

130 _____. "Zur Topographie und städtebaulichen Entwicklung von Ephesos." JÖAI 46 (1961-1963):136-57.

_____. See nos. 42, 1055.

131 Bammer, Anton; Brein, Friedrich; and Wolff, Petra.
"Das Tieropfer am Artemisaltar von Ephesos." In

Studien zur Religion und Kultur Kleinasiens. Festschrift für Friedrich Karl Dörner zum 65. Geburtstag am 28. Februar 1976. Edited by S. Şahin, E.
Schwertheim, and J. Wagner. EPRO, 66.1. Leiden:
E. J. Brill, 1978, 1:107-57.

132 Bammer, Anton; Fleischer, Robert; and Knibbe, Dieter.
Führer durch das Archäologische Museum in Selçuk-
Ephesos. Vienna: Österreichisches Archäologisches
Institut, 1974.

133 Bankó, Julius. Ausstellung von Fundstücken aus
Ephesos im Unterem Belvedere. 4th ed. Führer
durch die kunsthistorischen Sammlungen in Wien, 5.
Vienna: Druck J. Weiner, 1927.

134 Baran, Musa. Ephesus and its Surroundings. Izmir:
Molay Matbaacilik, n.d.

_____. See nos. 471, 472.

135 Barnett, R. D. "Early Greek and Oriental Ivories."
Journal of Hellenic Studies 68 (1948):1-25.

136 Başaran, Sait. "Konservierung und Restaurierung eines
Glasmosaiks in Ephesos." In Lebendige Altertumswissenschaft. Festgabe zur Vollendung des 70. Lebensjahres von Hermann Vetters dargebracht von Freunden, Schülern und Kollegen. Vienna: Verlag Adolf
Holzhausens Nfg., 1985, pp. 403-04.

137 Batiffol, P. "Inscription chrétienne d'Ephèse." Bulletin
de la Société nationale des antiquaires de France
(1923):292-93.

Baus, Karl. See no. 1458.

138 Bayral, Mete. Secret Ephesus. Izmir: Ofis Ticaret
Matbaacilik San. Ltd. Sti, 1985.

139 Bean, George E. Aegean Turkey. 2nd ed. London:
Ernest Benn, 1979, pp. 128-50.

140 _____. Aegean Turkey, An Archaeological Guide.
London: Ernest Benn Limited, 1966, pp. 160-84.

141 Bees, Nikos A. "Forschungen in Ephesos." Byzan-
     tinisch-neugriechische Jahrbücher 5 (1926-1927):
     497-99.

142 Benedum, J. "Titos Statilios Kriton. Ein Beitrag zur
     medizin-historischen Epigraphik der Antike." Clio
     Medica 7 (1972):249-58.

143 Benndorf, Otto. "Antike Baumodelle." JÖAI 5 (1902):
     175-95.

144 _____. "Bericht für archäologische Erforschung
     Kleinasiens." Anz. Wien 32 (1895):103-05.

145 _____. "Bericht über die österreichischen Ausgrabun-
     gen in Ephesus." Anz. Wien 34 (1897):12-30.

146 _____. "Erzstatue eines griechischen Athleten." In
     Forschungen in Ephesos. Vienna: Alfred Hölder,
     1906, 1:181-204.

147 _____. "Nachträge." JÖAI 3 (1900):Beibl. 221-24.

148 _____. "Nachträge." JÖAI 6 (1903):Beibl. 88-90.

149 _____. "Topographische Urkunde aus Ephesos." In
     Beiträge zur alten Geschichte und Geographie.
     Festschrift für Heinrich Kiepert. Berlin: Verlag von
     Dietrich Reimer, 1898, pp. 243-57.

150 _____. "Topographische Urkunde aus Ephesos."
     JÖAI 2 (1899):Beibl. 15-36.

151 _____. "Vorläufige Berichte über die Ausgrabungen
     in Ephesus, I." JÖAI 1 (1898):Beibl. 53-72.

152 _____. "Zur Ortskunde und Stadtgeschichte." In
     Forschungen in Ephesos. Vienna: Alfred Hölder,
     1906, 1:9-110.

153 Benndorf, Otto, and Wilberg, Wilhelm. "Studien am
     Artemision." In Forschungen in Ephesos. Vienna:
     Alfred Hölder, 1906, 1:205-34.

154 Bennett, Florence M. Religious Cults Associated with

the Amazons. New York: Columbia University Press, 1912, pp. 30-39.

155 Bérard, Jean. "Recherches sur les itinéraires de Saint Paul en Asie Mineure." Revue archéologique 6th ser. 5 (1935):57-90.

156 Berchem, Denis van. "La gérousie d'Ephèse." Museum Helveticum 37 (1980):25-40.

157 _____. "Trois cas d'asylie archaïque." Museum Helveticum 17 (1960):21-33.

158 Bernardi Ferrero, Daria De. "San Giovani di Efeso." Corsi di cultura sull'arte ravennate e bizantina 30 (1983):93-113.

159 _____. Teatri Classici in Asia Minore. Rome: "L'Erma" die Bretschneider, 1970, 3:37-66.

160 Bernhard, Oscar. "Der Sonnengott auf griechischen und römischen Münzen." Schweizerische numismatische Rundschau 25 (1933):245-98.

Bernhard-Walcher, Alfred. See no. 1055.

161 Berthiaume, G. "Helléniques III,4,17 et le sens du terme chalkeus à l'époque classique." Revue de philologie 48 (1974):304-7.

162 Betz, Artur. "Ephesia." Klio 52 (1970):27-32.

163 Bieber, Margarete. "Der Chiton der ephesischen Amazonen." Jahrbuch des Deutschen Archäologischen Instituts 33 (1918):49-75.

164 _____. Die Denkmäler zum Theaterwesen im Altertum. Berlin: Walter de Gruyter and Co., 1920, pp. 38-49.

165 _____. The History of the Greek and Roman Theater. Princeton: Princeton University Press, 1961.

Bilgi, Önder. See no. 787.

Blackman, D. J. See nos. 237, 238.

166 Blaiklock, Edward M. The Cities of the New Testament.
     London: Pickering and Inglis, 1965, pp. 62-68.

167 _____. "Ephesus." In Zondervan Pictorial Encyclo-
     pedia of the Bible. Edited by M. C. Tenney.
     Grand Rapids: Zondervan Publishing House, 1975,
     2:324-32.

168 _____. "Ephesus." In The New International Dic-
     tionary of Biblical Archaeology. Edited by E. M.
     Blaiklock and R. K. Harrison. Grand Rapids:
     Zondervan, 1983, p. 181.

169 Blanchet, Adrien. "Les statères d'or d'Ephèse."
     Procès-verbaux de la Société française de Numis-
     matique (1935-1936):14-16.

170 Blum, G. "Numismatique d'Antinoos." Journal inter-
     national d'Archéologie numismatique 16 (1914):33-70.

171 Boeckh, August. Corpus Inscriptionum Graecarum.
     vol. 2, pt. 14 "Inscriptiones Lydiae." Berlin: G.
     Reimer, 1843.

172 Börker, Christoph. "König Agesilaos von Sparta und
     der Artemis-Tempel in Ephesos." ZPE 37 (1980):
     69-75.

173 _____. "Eine pantheistische Weihung in Ephesos."
     ZPE 41 (1981):181-88.

174 Börker, Christoph, and Merkelbach, Reinhold, eds.,
     mit Hilfe von Engelmann, H., and Knibbe, D.
     Inschriften griechischer Städte aus Kleinasien.
     vol. XII: Die Inschriften von Ephesos. 2: Nr.
     101-599 (Repertorium). Bonn: Habelt, 1979.

175 _____. Inschriften griechischer Städte aus Kleinasien.
     vol. XV: Die Inschriften von Ephesos. 5: Nr.
     1446-2000 (Repertorium). Bonn: Habelt, 1980.

176 Bogaert, Raymond. Banques et banquiers dans les
     cités grecques. Leiden: A. W. Sijthoff, 1968.

177 Bollini, Maria. "Vibio Seneca." Studi Romagnoli 17
     (1966):229-35.

178 Bonanno, Anthony. Portraits and Other Heads on
     Roman Historical Relief up to the Age of Septimius
     Severus. British Archaeological Reports Supple-
     mentary Series, 6. Oxford: n.p., 1976, pp. 114-
     36; 205-08 (notes).

179 Bonnet, Jacques. Artemis d'Ephèse et la légende des
     Sept Dormants. Paris: Librairie Orientaliste Paul
     Geuthner, 1977.

180 Borchert, Gerald L. "Ephesus." In The International
     Standard Bible Encyclopedia. Edited by G. W.
     Bromiley. Grand Rapids: Wm. B. Eerdmans, 1982,
     2:115-17.

181 Borrell, H. P. "Restitution to the city of Ephesus
     (when called Arsinoe) of the coins hitherto attributed
     to Arsinoe in Cyreniaca, and to Arsinoe in Cilicia."
     Numismatic Chronicle 2 (1840):171-76.

182 Bosch, Clemens. "Die kleinasiatischen Münzen der
     römischen Kaiserzeit." Archäologischer Anzeiger
     (1931):422-25.

183 Bousquet, Jean. "Un hermès à Ephèse." Revue des
     études grecques 90 (1977):xvi.

184 _____. "L'hermès de Scopas à Ephèse." Revue de
     philologie 51 (1977):22-24.

185 Bowersock, Glen W. Greek Sophists in the Roman Em-
     pire. Oxford: Clarendon Press, 1969.

186 _____. "Plutarch and the Sublime Hymn of Ofellius
     Laetus." Greek, Roman, and Byzantine Studies 23
     (1982):275-79.

187 Bowie, E. L. "The 'Temple of Hadrian' at Ephesus."
     ZPE 8 (1971):137-41.

188 _____. "The Vedii Antonini and the Temple of
     Hadrian at Ephesus." In The Proceedings of the Xth
     International Congress of Classical Archaeology.
     Edited by E. Akurgal. Ankara: Türk Tarih Kurumu
     Basimevi, 1978, 2:867-74.

189 Boyd, Daniel A. "Ephesus." In The Interpreter's
    Dictionary of the Bible. Supplementary Volume.
    Edited by K. Crim. Nashville: Abingdon, 1976,
    pp. 269-71.

190 Brandes, W. "Ephesos in byzantinischer Zeit." Klio
    64 (1982):611-22.

191 Breglia, Laura. "Interrogativi sulle 'creseidi.'"
    Annali della Scuola Normale Superiore di Pisa 3rd
    ser. 4 (1974):659-86.

192 _____. "Il materiale proveniente dalla base centrale
    dell'Artemision di Efeso e le Monete di Lidia."
    Annali dell'Istituto Italiano di Numismatica 18-19
    (1971-1972):9-23.

193 Brein, Friedrich. "Ear studs for Greek Ladies."
    Anatolian Studies 32 (1982):89-92.

194 _____. "Geometrisch dekorierte Keramik aus Ephesos."
    Proceedings of the Xth International Congress of
    Classical Archaeology. Edited by E. Akurgal. Ankara:
    Türk Tarih Kurumu Basimevi, 1978, 2:721-28.

195 _____. "Zur ephesischen Topographie." JÖAI 51
    (1976-1977):Beibl. 65-76.

    _____. See no. 131.

196 Brenk, Beat. "Die Datierung der Reliefs am Hadrian-
    stempel in Ephesos und das Problem der tetrarchischen
    Skulptur des Ostens." Istanbuler Mitteilungen 18
    (1968):238-58.

197 Bringmann, Klaus. "Edikt der Triumvirn oder Senat-
    beschluss? Zu einem Neufund aus Ephesos."
    Epigraphica Anatolica 2 (1983):47-76.

198 Brockhoff, Wilhelm. Studien zur Geschichte der Stadt
    Ephesos vom IV. nachchristlichen Jahrhundert bis zu
    ihrem Untergang in der ersten Hälfte des XV. Jahr-
    hunderts. Jena: Universitäts-Buchdruckerei G.
    Neuenhahn, 1905.

199 Broughton, Thomas Robert S. "Roman Asia." In An
     Economic Survey of Ancient Rome. Edited by T.
     Frank. Baltimore: Johns Hopkins Press, 1938,
     4:503-916.

200 _____. "A Significant Break in the Cistophoric
     Coinage of Asia." AJA 41 (1937):248-49.

201 Bruce, Frederick F. "St. John at Ephesus." Bulletin
     of the John Rylands Library 60 (1978):339-61.

202 Bruns, Gerda. "Fragen zum Kopfschmuck kleinasiatisch-
     jonischer Priesterinnen." Kleinasian und Byzanz.
     Gesammelte Aufsätze zur Altertumskunde und Kunst-
     geschichte. Istanbuler Forschungen, 17. Berlin:
     Walter de Gruyter & Co., 1950, pp. 30-34.

203 _____. "Ein spätantikes Kopffragment aus Ephesos."
     In Studies Presented to David Moore Robinson on his
     seventieth Birthday. Edited by G. E. Mylonas.
     Saint Louis: Washington University, 1951, 1:688-93.

204 Buckler, William H. "Labour Disputes in the Province
     of Asia." In Anatolian Studies Presented to Sir
     William Mitchell Ramsay. Edited by W. H. Buckler
     and W. M. Calder. Manchester: University Press,
     1923, pp. 27-50.

205 _____. "T. Statilius Crito, Traiani Aug. medicus."
     JÖAI 30 (1937):Beibl. 5-8.

206 Budde, Ludwig. "Die vogelträgenden Priesterinnen der
     ephesischen Artemis und ihre östlichen Vorbild."
     Islam 39 (1964):8-13.

207 Bürchner, L. "Ephesos." In Paulys Realencyclopädie
     der classischen Altertumswissenschaft. Edited by G.
     Wissowa. Stuttgart: J. B. Metzlersche Verlags-
     buchhandlung, 1905, 5.2:2773-2822.

208 Büyükkolanci, Mustafa. "St. Jean Bazilikasi Atriumu."
     Efes Müzesi Yilliği 2 (1973-1978):38-45.

209 _____. "Zwei neugefundene Bauten der Johannes-

basilika von Ephesos: Baptisterium und Skeuophylakion." Istanbuler Mitteilungen 32 (1982):236-57.

210 Büyükkolanci, Mustafa; Içten, Cengiz; and Nollé, Johannes. "Einige Inschriften aus Ephesos." ZPE 40 (1980):256-58.

Büyükkolanci, Pervin. See no. 216.

211 Buluç, Sevim. "Belevi Mezar Aniti." In VII. Türk Tarih Kongresi, 1:137-44. Türk Tarih Kurumu yayinlarindan, 9. seri, no. 7. Ankara: Türk Tarih Kurumu Basimevi, 1972.

212 _____. "The Tomb Monument at Belevi near Ephesos." In The Proceedings of the Xth International Congress of Classical Archaeology. Edited by E. Akurgal. Ankara: Türk Tarih Kurumu Basimevi, 1978, 2:1085-92.

213 Burrell, Barbara. "Neokoroi: Greek Cities of the Roman East." Dissertation, Harvard University, 1980.

214 Butler, Howard C. "The Elevated Columns at Sardis and the Sculptured Pedestals from Ephesus." In Anatolian Studies Presented to Sir William Mitchell Ramsay. Edited by W. H. Buckler and W. M. Calder. Manchester: Manchester University Press, 1923, pp. 51-57.

215 Canbaş, Yaşar. "Efes Müzesindeki Efes Arili Sikkeleri." Efes Harabeleri ve Müzesi Yilliği 1 (1972):99-104.

216 Canbaş, Yaşar and Büyükkolanci, Pervin. "1976 Yilinda Çeşitli Yollarla Efes Müzesine Gelen Envanterlik Sikkeler." Efes Müzesi Yilliği 2 (1973-78): 46-55.

217 Cantarelli, Luigi. "Un curator Tiberis in una lapide Greca di Efeso." Bulletin Communal 35 (1907):108-114.

Carson, Robert A. G. See no. 1328.

218 Castelfranchi, M. "Il battistero della chiesa di San
    Giovanni ad Efeso (Ayasoluk)." In Actes du 15.
    Congrès international d'études byzantines. Athens:
    1976, 2:129-42.

219 Ceroni, E. "Grande Artemide degli Efesini! Il tumulto
    degli Efesini contro San Paolo alla luce delle recenti
    scoperte archeologiche (Atti 19:24-40)." Scuola
    Cattolica 60.4 (1932):121-42; 203-26.

220 Champlin, Edward. "Hadrian's Heir." ZPE 21 (1976):
    79-89.

221 Chapouthier, Fernand. "La coiffe d'Artémis dans
    Ephèse trois fois néocore." Revue des études
    anciennes 40 (1938):125-32.

222 _____. Les Dioscures au service d'une déesse. Etude
    d'iconographie religieuse. Paris: E. de Boccard,
    1935, pp. 31-33, 74-77.

223 Charneux, Pierre. "Liste argienne de Théarodoques."
    Bulletin de correspondance hellénique 90 (1966):
    198-206.

224 Chishull, Edmund. Antiquitates Asiaticae Christianam
    Aeram Antecedents. London: G. Bowyer, 1728.

225 Chiţescu, Maria. "A propos des monnaies frappées
    par Marc-Antoine pour ses légions." Dacia n.s. 18
    (1974):147-53.

226 Clarke, Hyde. Ephesus. Being a Lecture Delivered at
    Smyrna. Smyrna: G. Green, 1863.

227 Clarke, J. G. A. "Ephèse, la Basilique St.-Jean
    l'Evangeliste, élevée sous Justinien et la Basilique
    Sainte-Marie, lieu de réunion du IIIe Concile en
    431." Bible et Terre Sainte 51 (1961):6-18.

228 Clemen, Carl. "The Sojourn of the Apostle John at
    Ephesus." American Journal of Theology 9 (1905):
    643-76.

229 Cody, Jane M. "New Evidence for the Republican Aedes
    Vestae." AJA 77 (1973):43-50.

230 Coleman, John R. "A Roman Terracotta Figurine of the Ephesian Artemis in the McDaniel Collection." Harvard Studies in Classical Philology 70 (1965): 111-15.

231 Conybeare, William J., and Howson, John S. The Life and Letters of St. Paul. Reprint ed. Grand Rapids: Wm. B. Eerdmans, 1968, pp. 368-74; 419-33.

232 Conze, Alexander. "Hermes-Kadmilos." Mitteilungen des Deutschen Archäologischen Instituts (Athenische Abteilung) 13 (1888):202-06.

233 Cook, Arthur B. "The Bee in Greek Mythology." Journal of Hellenic Studies 15 (1895):1-24.

234 _____. Zeus. A Study in Ancient Religion. Cambridge: Cambridge University Press, 1914-1940, 3 vols.

235 Cook, Brian F. "The Tympanum of the Fourth-Century Temple of Artemis at Ephesus." British Museum Quarterly 37 (1973):137-40.

236 Cook, J. M. "Greek Archaeology in Western Asia Minor." Journal of Hellenic Studies. Archaeological Report for 1959-60 (1960):46.

237 Cook, J. M., and Blackman, D. J. "Archaeology in Western Asia Minor 1965-70." The Journal of Hellenic Studies. Archaeological Reports for 1970-71 17 (1971):41-43.

238 _____. "Greek Archaeology in Western Asia Minor." The Journal of Hellenic Studies. Archaeological Reports for 1964-65 (1965):46-49.

238a Coreth, Emerich. Zur Logoslehre von Heraklit bis Johannes. Vienna: Gesellschaft der Freunde von Ephesos, 1982.

239 Cowper, H. S. "Three Bronze Figures from Asia Minor. II. A Bronze Figure of Artemis from Ephesos." The Journal of Hellenic Studies 29 (1909):195-96.

240 Curtius, Carl. "Inschriften aus Ephesos." Hermes 4
      (1870):174-228.

241 _____. "Inschriften aus Kleinasien. A. Ephesos."
      Hermes 7 (1873):28-46.

242 _____. "Sculpturen aus Ephesos." Archäologische
      Zeitung 26 (1868):81-83.

243 Curtius, Ernst. "Beiträge zur Geschichte und Topo-
      graphie Kleinasiens (Ephesos, Pergamon, Smyrna,
      Sardes)." Abhandlungen der Preussischen Akademie
      der Wissenschaften zu Berlin (Philosophisch-
      historische Klasse) (1872):1-91.

244 _____. Ephesos. Ein Vortrag. Berlin: Verlag von
      Wilhelm Hertz, 1874.

245 _____. "Die Säulenreliefs von Ephesos." Archäo-
      logische Zeitung 30 (1872):72-74.

246 Curtius, Ludwig. "Redeat Narratio." Mitteilungen des
      Deutschen Archäologischen Instituts 4 (1951):10-34.

247 Czermiński, X. M. Wyprawa na Patmos, Efez i Kretę.
      Kraków: Czcionkami Drukarni "Czasu," 1904, pp.
      65-142.

248 Danish National Museum. The Royal Collection of Coins
      and Medals. Sylloge nummorum Graecorum. Copen-
      hagen: E. Munksgaard, 1942- .

249 Danker, Frederick W. Benefactor: Epigraphic Study
      of a Graeco-Roman and New Testament Semantic Field.
      St. Louis: Clayton Publishing House, Inc., 1982,
      nos. 8; 45; 46.

250 Da Scandiano, F. Efesos pagana-cristiana. Guida
      Illustrata. Regio Emilia: Frate Francesco, 1932.

251 Daux, Georges. "Décret d'Ephèse pour un vainqueur
      aux Isthmia et aux Néméa." ZPE 28 (1978):41-47.

252 _____. "Sur une dédicace macédonienne à Artémis
Ephésia." Bulletin de correspondance hellénique 83
(1959):549-52.

253 Dawid, Maria. "Bemerkungen zu zwei Relieffriessen
aus dem ephesischen Elfenbeinfund." In Forschungen
und Funde-Festschrift Bernhard Neutsch. Edited by
F. Krinzinger, B. Otto, and E. Walde-Psenner.
Innsbrucker Beiträge zur Kulturwissenschaft, 21.
Innsbruck: Institut für Sprachwissenschaft der
Universität Innsbruck, 1980, pp. 95-102.

254 _____. "Drei römische Elfenbeinporträts aus Ephesos."
In Festschrift Otto R. v. Lutterotti. Innsbruck:
Österreichische Kommissionsbuchhandlung in Komm.,
1973, pp. 43-51.

255 _____. "Die rundplastischen Schnitzereien aus dem
ephesischen Elfenbeinfund." In Pro Arte Antiqua.
Festschrift für Hedwig Kenner. Sonderschriften
herausgegeben vom Österreichischen Archäologischen
Institut, 18. Vienna: Verlag A. F. Koska, 1982,
1:49-53.

256 _____. Weltwunder der Antike. Baukunst und
Plastik. Frankfurt: Umschau-Verlag, 1968.

257 Dawid, Maria, and Dawid, Paul G. "Restaurierungsarbeiten von 1965-1970." JÖAI 50 (1972-1975):Grabun-
gen in Ephesos von 1960-1969 bzw. 1970, 525-58.

Dawid, Paul G. See no. 257.

258 Debord, Pierre. Aspects sociaux et économiques de la
vie religieuse dans l'Anatolie gréco-romaine. EPRO,
88. Leiden: E. J. Brill, 1982.

259 Deichmann, I. W. "Zur spätantiken Bauplastik von
Ephesus." In Mélanges Mansel. Türk Tarih Kurumu
Yayinlari, Dizi 7, Sa. 60. Ankara: Türk Tarih
Kurumu Basimevi, 1974, 1:549-70.

260 Deininger, Jürgen. Die Provinziallandtage der
römischen Kaiserzeit von Augustus bis zum Ende des
dritten Jahrhunderts n. Chr. Vestigia. Beiträge

zur alten Geschichte, 6. Berlin: C. H. Beck'sche Verlagsbuchhandlung, 1965.

261 Deissmann, Adolf. "Die Ausgrabungen in Ephesus." Antiquitäten Rundschau 29 (1931):440-42.

262 _____. "Die Ausgrabungen in Ephesos 1926." Theologische Blätter 6 (1927):17-20.

263 _____. "Ephesia Grammata." In Abhandlungen zur semitischen Religionskunde und Sprachwissenschaft. Wolf Wilhelm Grafen von Baudissin. Giessen: Adolf Töpelmann Verlag, 1918, pp. 121-24.

264 _____. "The Excavations in Ephesus." Biblical Review 15 (1930):332-46.

265 _____. "Der Wiederbeginn der Ausgrabungen in Ephesos." Archäologischer Anzeiger 42 (1927):170-74.

266 _____. "Das wiedererstehende Ephesos." Die Woche 11 (1927):297-99.

267 Delehaye, Hippolyte. "Les actes de Saint Timothée." In Anatolian Studies Presented to William Hepburn Buckler. Edited by W. M. Calder and J. Keil. Manchester: University Press, 1939, pp. 77-84.

268 Demus, Otto. "Graphische Elemente in der spätantiken Plastik." In Tortulae. Studien zu altchristlichen und byzantinischen Monumenten. Edited by W. N. Schumacher. Römische Quartalschrift für christliche Altertumskunde und Kirchengeschichte, Supplementheft, 30. Rome: Herder, 1966, pp. 77-81.

269 Deonna, W. "Histoire d'un emblème, la couronne murale des villes et pays personnifiés." Genava 18 (1940): 119-236.

270 _____. "Trois statuettes d'Artémis éphésienne." Revue archéologique 5th ser. 19 (1924):5-23.

271 d'Este, G. La Diana Efesina. Congetture sul vero suo significato. Rome: 1845.

272 Detschew, Dimiter. "Artemis." In Reallexikon für
Antike und Christentum. Edited by Th. Klauser.
Stuttgart: Hiersemann Verlags, 1950, 1:714-18.

273 Deutsch, Bernard F. Our Lady of Ephesus. Milwaukee:
The Bruce Publishing Co., 1965.

274 Devambez, Pierre. "Les Amazones et l'Orient." Revue
archéologique (1976):265-80.

275 _____. "Le groupe statuaire des Amazones à Ephèse."
Comptes rendus de l'Académie des Inscriptions et
Belles-Lettres (1976):162-70.

276 Devijver, H. "Ein Bleigewicht mit Agoranomeninschrift
aus Metropolis." ZPE 50 (1983):270-74.

277 Dickings, G. "Damophon of Messese, II." Annual of
the British School at Athens 13 (1906-1970):356-99.

278 Diehl, Charles. "Note sur deux inscriptions byzantines
d'Ephèse." Comptes rendus de l'Académie des Inscriptions et Belles-Lettres (1908):207-13.

279 Diez, Erna. "Der Flussgott mit der Tierpranke." In
Mosaïque. Recueil d'hommages à Henri Stern. Paris:
Editions Recherche sur les civilisations, 1983, pp.
109-113.

280 _____. "Isis-Alexandria auf dem grossen Fries von
Ephesos." In Alessandria e il mondo ellenistico-
romano. Studi in onore Achille Adriani. Rome:
"L'ERMA" di Bretschneider, 1983, pp. 155-61.

281 _____. "Die Repräsentantinnen der Stadt Ephesos."
In Lebendige Altertumswissenschaft. Festgabe zur
Vollendung des 70. Lebensjahres von Hermann Vetters
dargebracht von Freunden, Schülern und Kollegen.
Vienna: Verlag Adolf Holzhausens Nfg., 1985, pp.
216-19.

282 Dörner, Friedrich K. Der Erlass des Statthalters von
Asia Paullus Fabius Persicus. Greifswald: Buch-
druckerei Hans Adler, 1935.

283 Dörpfeld, Wilhelm. "Das Theater von Ephesos."
Archäologischer Anzeiger 28 (1913):37-42.

284 _____. "Das Theater von Ephesos." Berliner
philologische Wochenschrift 33 (1913):1340-43.

285 Dohrn, Tobias. "Altes und Neues über die ephesischen
Amazonen." Jahrbuch des Deutschen Archäologischen
Instituts 94 (1979):112-26.

286 Domaszewski, A. V. "Die ephesische Inschrift des
Marcus Claudius Pupienus Maximus." In Festschrift
Theodor Gomperz dargebracht zum siebzigsten
Geburtstage. Vienna: Alfred Hölder, 1902, pp.
233-36.

287 _____. "Ephesische Inschrift eines Tribunen der
Legio VI Macedonica." JÖAI 2 (1899):Beibl. 81-86.

288 Dressler, Wolfgang. "Karoide Inschriften im Steinbruch
von Belevi." JÖAI 48 (1966-1967):73-76.

289 Drew-Bear, Thomas. "Representations of Temples on the
Greek Imperial Coinage." American Numismatic Society Museum Notes 19 (1974):27-63.

290 Drexler, Wilhelm. "Der Isis-und Sarapis-Cultus in
Kleinasien." Numismatische Zeitschrift 21 (1889):
78-94, 390.

291 Dulière, C. "Rapports entre l'iconographie de
Télèphe et de la biche et celle des jumeaux et de
la louve." Bulletin de l'Institut historique belge de
Rome 42 (1972):73-98.

292 Dunand, Françoise. Le culte d'Isis dans le bassin
oriental de la Méditerranée. EPRO, 26.2-3. Leiden:
E. J. Brill, 1973.

293 Dunst, Günter. "Zur samischen Artemis." Chiron 2
(1972):191-200.

294 Duyuran, Rüstem. Ephèse. Ankara: Direction
générale de la presse, 1951.

295 _____. Ephesos Kilavuzu. Istanbul: Millî Eğitim
Basimevi, 1950.

296 Easter, John. "Among the Ruins of Ephesus."
Records of the Past 5 (1906):111-16.

297 Ebert, Joachim. "dosis olige te phile te (zur
Athletenehrung Ephesos II Nr. 72)." ZPE 35
(1979):293-96.

298 _____. "Zum Epigramm auf den Schwerathleten
Aurelios Achilleus aus Aphrodisias." Stadion.
Zeitschrift für Geschichte des Sports und der
Körperkultur 7.2 (1981):203-10.

299 Eck, Werner. "Epigraphische Untersuchungen zu
Konsuln und Senatoren des 1.-3. Jh. n. Ch." ZPE
37 (1980):31-68.

300 _____. "Zu drei ephesischen Inschriften." ZPE 14
(1974):163-67.

301 _____. "Zur Verwaltungsgeschichte Italiens unter
Marc Aurel-Ein Iuridicus per Flaminiam et Trans-
padanam." ZPE 8 (1971):71-79.

302 Eck, Werner, and Merkelbach, Reinhold. "Inschrift
für einen Senator aus dem Kaystrostal." ZPE 33
(1979):148.

303 Efes harabeleri. Izmir ve Havalisi Asariatika Muhipleri
Cemiyeti, no. 1. Izmir, n.d.

304 Egger, Rudolf. "Die Ämterlaufbahn des M. Nonius
Macrinus." JÖAI 9 (1906):Beibl. 61-76.

305 Eichler, Fritz. "Ein augusteisches Denkmal in
Ephesos." Wiener Studien 79 (1966):592-97.

306 _____. "Der Bronzeathlet aus Ephesos." Mitteilungen des Vereins der Freunde des humanistischen
Gymnasiums (Wien) 2 (1957):3-5.

307 _____. "Der Bronzeathlet aus Ephesus in verbesserter Wiederherstellung." Anz. Wien 88 (1951):373.

308 _____. "Die Bronzestatue aus Ephesos, in verbesserter Wiederherstellung." Jahrbuch der kunsthistorischen Sammlungen in Wien 50 (1953):15-22.

309 _____. "Das Denkmal des Eutropius von Ephesos." Anz. Wien 76 (1939):5-13.

310 _____. "Ephesos: Ausgrabungen 1964 und 1965." Fasti Archaeologici 18-19 (1963-1964):421-22.

311 _____. "Ephesos Bericht über die österreichischen Grabungen 1967." Türk Arkeoloji Dergisi 16.2 (1967):93-98.

312 _____. "Ephesos. Grabungsbericht 1968." Anz. Wien 106 (1969):131-46.

313 _____. "Ephesus, 1966. Recent Archaeological Research in Turkey." Anatolian Studies 17 (1967):30.

314 _____. "Ephesus, 1967. Recent Archaeological Research in Turkey." Anatolian Studies 18 (1968):39.

315 _____. "Ephesus, 1968. Recent Archaeological Research in Turkey." Anatolian Studies 19 (1969):18-19.

316 _____. "Ephesos-Vorläufiger Grabungsbericht." Anz. Wien 98 (1961):65-73.

317 _____. "Fragmente attischer Sarkophage in Wien." JÖAI 36 (1946):82-96.

318 _____. "Ein Jahrfünft österreichischer Arbeit in Ephesos." Bustan 9 (1968):89-94.

319 _____. "Karische Aphrodite und ephesische Artemis. Berichtigungen und Nachträge." JÖAI 42 (1955): Beibl. 1-22.

320 _____. Meisterwerke in Wien. Zwei Athletenstatuen. Vienna: Julius Bard, 1922.

321 _____. "Eine neue Amazone und andere Skulpturen aus dem Theater von Ephesos." JÖAI 43 (1956-1958): 7-18.

322 _____. "Nochmals die Sphinxgruppe aus Ephesos (zu ÖJh XXX 1937 S. 75ff)." JÖAI 45 (1960):5-22.

323 _____. "Die österreichischen Ausgrabungen in Ephesos." Anz. Wien 105 (1968):79-95.

324 _____. "Die österreichischen Ausgrabungen in Ephesos im Jahre 1960." Anz. Wien 98 (1961):65-74.

325 _____. "Die österreichischen Ausgrabungen in Ephesos im Jahre 1961." Anz. Wien 99 (1962):37-53.

326 _____. "Die österreichischen Ausgrabungen in Ephesos im Jahre 1962." Anz. Wien 100 (1963):45-59.

327 _____. "Die österreichischen Ausgrabungen in Ephesos im Jahre 1963." Anz. Wien 101 (1964):39-44.

328 _____. "Die österreichischen Ausgrabungen in Ephesos im Jahre 1964." Anz. Wien 102 (1965):93-109.

329 _____. "Die österreichischen Ausgrabungen in Ephesos im Jahre 1965." Anz. Wien 103 (1966):7-16.

330 _____. "Die österreichischen Ausgrabungen in Ephesos im Jahre 1966." Anz. Wien 104 (1967):15-28.

331 _____. "Die österreichischen Ausgrabungen in Ephesos im Jahre 1967." Anz. Wien 105 (1968):79-95.

332 _____. "Römisches Frauenbildnis aus Ephesos." Wiener humanistische Blätter 4 (1961):22-23.

333 _____. "Thebanische Sphinx. Ein Bildwerk aus Ephesos." JÖAI 30 (1937):75-110.

334 _____. "Türkei/Ephesos." JÖAI 47 (1964-1965): Grabungen 1965, 5-12.

335 _____. "Türkei/Ephesos." JÖAI 47 (1966): Grabungen 1966, 3-7.

336 _____. "Türkei/Ephesos." JÖAI 48 (1966-1967):
Grabungen 1967, 3-7.

337 _____. "Türkei/Ephesos." JÖAI 49 (1968-1971):
Grabungen 1968, 13-18.

338 _____. "Weibliche Porträtstatue aus Ephesos."
JÖAI 37 (1948):49-52.

339 _____. "Zu Bronzen aus Ephesos." JÖAI 24 (1929):
198-219.

340 _____. (+) "Zum Partherdenkmal von Ephesos."
JÖAI 49 (1971):Beih. 2, 102-136.

341 _____. "Zur Sphinxgruppe aus Ephesos." Anz.
Wien 96 (1959):213.

_____. See no. 1502.

342 Eichler, Fritz; Seiterle, S.; and Kasper, Sándor.
"Ephesos." JÖAI 47 (1964-1965):Grabungen 1966,
3-16.

343 Ekschmitt, Werner. Die Sieben Weltwunder, ihre
Erbauung, Zerstörung und Wiederentdeckung. Mainz:
Verlag Philipp von Zabern, 1984.

344 Elderkin, George W. "The bee of Artemis." American
Journal of Philology 60 (1939):203-13.

345 _____. "Sambin's Ephesian Diana." Art in America
27 (1939):22-8.

345a Elliger, Winfried. Ephesos. Geschichte einer antiken
Weltstadt. Stuttgart: Kohlhammer, 1985.

Emminghaus, Johannes H. See no. 1458.

346 Emmrich, Kurt. Frühe Stätten der Christenheit.
Munich: Kösel-Verlag, 1955, pp. 124-66.

347 Engelmann, Helmut. "Abschriften von Otto Benndorf."
Epigraphica Anatolica 2 (1983):21-24.

348 _____. "Die Bauinschriften des Prytaneions in
Ephesos." In Lebendige Altertumswissenschaft.
Festgabe zur Vollendung des 70. Lebensjahres von
Hermann Vetters dargebracht von Freunden, Schülern
und Kollegen. Vienna: Verlag Adolf Holzhausens
Nfg., 1985, pp. 155-57.

349 _____. "C. Iulius Kleon aus Eumeneia." ZPE 20
(1976):86.

350 _____. "Eine christliche Inschrift." ZPE 10 (1973):
86.

351 _____. "Inschrift und Literatur." ZPE 51 (1983):
123-30.

352 _____. "Inschriften aus Ephesos." ZPE 24 (1977):
201-04.

353 _____. "Inschriften aus Ephesos." ZPE 31 (1978):
225-26.

353a _____. "Statue und Standort." In Römische
Geschichte, Altertumskunde und Epigraphik. Fest-
schrift für Artur Betz zur Vollendung seines 80.
Lebensjahres. Edited by E. Weber and G. Dobesch.
Archäologisch-Epigraphische Studien, 1. Vienna:
Selbstverlag der Österreichischen Gesellschaft für
Archäologie, 1985, pp. 249-55.

354 _____. "Der Tempel des Hadrian in Ephesos und der
Proconsul Servaeus Innocens." ZPE 9 (1972):91-96.

355 _____. "Zu einem Brief von Attalos II." ZPE 19
(1975):224.

356 _____. "Zu einer Inschrift aus Ephesos." ZPE 19
(1975):134.

357 _____. "Zu Inschriften aus Ephesos." ZPE 26
(1977):154-56.

358 _____. "Zum Archivwesen von Ephesos." ZPE 22
(1976):84.

359 _____. "Zum Gedicht der Prytanin Claudia Trophime."
ZPE 36 (1979):90.

360 _____. "Zum Pollionymphäum in Ephesos." ZPE 10
(1973):89-90.

_____. See nos. 765, 1453, 1454.

361 Engelmann, Helmut, and Knibbe, Dieter. "Aus
ephesischen Skizzenbüchern." JÖAI 52 (1978-1980):
19-61.

362 Engelmann, Helmut; Knibbe, Dieter; and Merkelbach,
Reinhold. Inschriften griechischer Städte aus
Kleinasien. vol. XIII: Die Inschriften von Ephesos.
3: Nr. 600-1000 (Repertorium). Bonn: Habelt,
1980.

363 _____. Inschriften griechischer Städte aus Kleinasien.
vol. XIV: Die Inschriften von Ephesos. 4: Nr.
1001-1445 (Repertorium). Bonn: Habelt, 1980.

364 "Ephesos. Die Aufdeckung des antiken Ephesos."
Antiquitäten-Rundschau 26 (1928):332.

365 Die Ephesosgrabung ihren Förderen und Freunden als
Dank und Bitte anno 1959. n.c.: n.p., n.d.

366 Erdogan, H. Iyon Medeniyeti ve Efes. Aydin Halkevi
Nesriyati, no. 11. Aydin, 1935.

Erim, Kenan. See no. 16.

367 Ervine, St John. "John Turtle Wood, discoverer of the
Artemision 1869." Isis 28 (1938):376-84.

368 Euzet, J. "Remarques sur 'Jérusalem?--Ephèse?' de Cl.
Kopp." Divus Thomas 60 (1957):47-72.

369 Fabbrini, Laura. "Addenda Iconografica. Tre nuove
attribuzioni per la iconografia di Druso Maggiore."
Bollettino d'Arte 52 (1967):67-69.

370 Falconer, Th. "Observations on Pliny's Account of the
Temple of Diana at Ephesus." Archaeologia 11,2
(1808):1-21.

371 Falkener, Edward. Ephesus and the Temple of Diana.
London: Day & Son, 1862.

372 _____. "Letter from Edward Falkener upon the So-
Called Tomb of St. Luke at Ephesus." Transactions
of the Society of Biblical Archaeology 7 (1882):241-47.

373 Falwell, Reuben H. "The place of Ephesus in the Pro-
pagation of Christianity in New Testament Times."
Dissertation, Southern Baptist Theological Seminary,
1948.

374 Fasolo, Furio. L'architettura romana di Efeso.
Bollettino del Centro di studi per la storia dell'
architettura, 18. Rome: Casa dei Crescenzi, 1962.

375 _____. "La Basilica del Concilio di Efeso." Fede e
Arte 7-8 (1958):280-308.

376 _____. "La basilica del Concilio di Efeso con alcune
note sull'architettura romana della valle del Mean-
dro." Palladio 6 (1956):1-30.

377 Fauth, W. "Gyges und die 'Falken.'" Hermes 96
(1968):257-64.

378 Fehr, Burkhard. "Archäologen, Techniker, Indus-
trielle. Betrachtungen zur Wiederaufstellung der
Bibliothek des Celsus in Ephesos." Hephaistos 3
(1981):107-25.

379 Felten, Florens. "Heiligtümer oder Märkte." Antike
Kunst 26 (1983):84-105.

380 Ferber, Elfriede. "Gross ist die Artemis der Epheser."
Troja, Ephesus, Milet. Merian. Das Monatsheft der
Städte und Landschaften, 12.19. Hamburg: Hoff-
mann und Campe Verlag, 1966, pp. 28-31.

381 Fergusson, James. "Observations on the preceding Paper
on the Temple of Diana at Ephesus." Transactions

of the Royal Institute of British Architects (1883-1884):171-74.

382 _____. "On the Temple of Diana at Ephesus and the Hypaethrum of the Greeks." Transactions of the Royal Institute of British Architects (1876-77):77-99.

383 _____. The Temple of Diana at Ephesus. London: Trübner & Co., 1883.

384 _____. "The temple of Diana at Ephesus, with special reference to Mr. Wood's discoveries of its remains." Transactions of the Royal Institute of British Architects (1882-1883):147-68.

385 Fergusson, James, and Wood, John T. "The Temple of Diana at Ephesus." Journal of Proceedings of the Royal Institute of British Architects (1884-1885):165ff.

386 Fiechter, Ernst R. Baugeschichtliche Entwicklung des antiken Theaters. Munich: C. H. Beck, 1914.

387 Filson, Floyd V. "Ephesus and the New Testament." Biblical Archaeologist 8 (1945):73-80.

388 Finegan, Jack. The Archaeology of the New Testament. The Mediterranean World of the Early Christian Apostles. London: Croom Helm, 1981, pp. 155-71.

389 _____. "Ephesus." In The Interpreter's Dictionary of the Bible. Edited by G. A. Buttrick. Nashville: Abingdon Press, 1962, 2:114-18.

390 _____. Light from the Ancient Past. The Archaeological Background of the Hebrew-Christian Religion. Princeton: Princeton University Press, 1959, 2:345-50.

391 Firneis, Maria; Hölbl, Günther, and Langmann, Gerhard. "Die ägyptische Wasserauslaufuhr aus Ephesos." JÖAI 55 (1984):Beibl. 4ff.

392 Fischer, Thomas. "Zwei Lots antiker Münzen." Münzen- und Medaillensammler Berichte aus allen Gebieten der Geld-Münzen-und Medaillenkunde 11 (1971):1171-76.

393 Flacelière, Robert; Robert, Jeanne; and Robert, Louis. "Ephèse." REG Bull. Epig. 52 (1938):nos. 361-64.

394 _____. "Ephèse." REG Bull. Epig. 53 (1939):nos. 336-38.

395 Fleischer, Robert. "Aphroditetorso vom Pollionymphaeum in Ephesos." JÖAI 49 (1971):Beih. 2, 165-71.

396 _____. "Artemis Ephesia." In Lexicon Iconographicum Mythologiae Classicae. Munich: Artemis Verlag, 1984, 2.1:755-63.

397 _____. "Artemis Ephesia und Aphrodite von Aphrodisias." In Die orientalischen Religionen im Römerreich. Edited by M. J. Vermaseren. EPRO, 93. Leiden: E. J. Brill, 1981, pp. 298-315.

398 _____. Artemis von Ephesos und verwandte Kultstatuen aus Anatolien und Syrien. EPRO, 35. Leiden: E. J. Brill, 1973.

399 _____. "Artemis von Ephesos und verwandte Kultstatuen aus Anatolien und Syrien. Supplement." In Studien zur Religion und Kultur Kleinasiens. Festschrift für Friedrich Karl Dörner zum 65. Geburtstag am 28. Februar 1976. Edited by S. Şahin, E. Schwertheim, and J. Wagner. EPRO, 66.1. Leiden: E. J. Brill, 1978, 1:324-58.

400 _____. "Artemisstatuette aus dem Hanghaus II in Ephesos." JÖAI 49 (1971):Beih. 2, 172-88.

401 _____. "Eine bekleidete Nachbildung der Artemis von Ephesos." JÖAI 52 (1978-1980):63-66.

402 _____. "Ergänzungen zum Abschnitt 'Der figürliche Schmuck.'" In Forschungen in Ephesos. vol. 6: Das Mausoleum von Belevi. Vienna: Österreichisches Archäologisches Institut, 1979, pp. 121-60.

403 _____. "Der Fries des Hadrianstempels in Ephesos." In Festschrift für Fritz Eichler zum achtzigsten Geburtstag. Vienna: Österreichisches Archäologisches Institut, 1967, pp. 23-71.

404 _____. "Eine neue Darstellung der doppelten Nemesis von Smyrna." In Hommages à Maarten J. Vermaseren. EPRO, 68. Leiden: E. J. Brill, 1978, 1:392-96.

405 _____. "Neues zu kleinasiatischen Kultstatuen." Archäologischer Anzeiger 98 (1983):81-93.

406 _____. "Skulpturenfunde." JÖAI 50 (1972-1975): Grabungen in Ephesos von 1960-1969 bzw. 1970, 421-68.

407 _____. "Späthellenistische Gruppe vom Pollionymphaeum in Ephesos mit dem Polyphemabenteuer des Odysseus." JÖAI 49 (1971):Beih. 2, 137-64.

408 _____. "Zu den trajanischen Elfenbeinfriesen aus Ephesos." Archäologischer Anzeiger (1983):539-41.

409 _____. "Zur Deutung des 'Diskophoros' Polyklets." JÖAI 52 (1978-1980):1-9.

410 _____. "Zwei eklektische Statuen aus Ephesos." In Pro Arte Antiqua. Festschrift für Hedwig Kenner. Sonderschriften herausgegeben vom Österreichischen Archäologischen Institut, 18. Vienna: Verlag A. F. Koska, 1982, 1:123-29.

_____. See no. 132.

411 Fogazza, Giovanni. "Per una storia della lega ionica." La Parola del Passato 28 (1973):155-69.

412 Fontrier, A. M. "Peri tes en Ionia Metropoleos." Mouseion kai Bibliotheke tes [en Smyrne] Euangelikes Scholes (1876-1878):65-101.

413 Forchheimer, Philipp. "Wasserleitungen." In Forschungen in Ephesos. Vienna: Österreichische Verlagsgesellschaft, 1923, 3:224-55.

414 Forrer, Leonard. The Weber Collection. vol. 3. Asia. London: Spink and Son, 1929.

415 Foss, Clive. "Archaeology and the 'Twenty Cities' of Byzantine Asia." AJA 81 (1977):469-86.

416 _____. "Byzantine Cities of Western Asia Minor."
Dissertation, Harvard University, 1972.

417 _____. Ephesus after Antiquity: A Late Antique,
Byzantine, and Turkish City. Cambridge: Cambridge University Press, 1979.

418 _____. "Three Apparent Early Examples of the Era
of Creation." ZPE 31 (1978):241-46.

419 Foss, Clive, and Magdalino, Paul. Rome and Byzantium.
The Making of the Past. Oxford: Elsevier-Phaidon,
1977, pp. 72-78.

420 Fossel, Elisabeth A. "Zum sogenannten Odeion in
Ephesos." In Festschrift für Fritz Eichler zum
achtzigsten Geburtstag. Vienna: Österreichisches
Archäologisches Institut, 1967, pp. 72-81.

421 _____. "Zum Tempel auf dem Staatsmarkt in Ephesos."
JÖAI 50 (1972-73):212-19.

422 Fossel, Elisabeth A., and Langmann, Gerhard. "Das
Nymphaeum des C. Laecanius Bassus in Ephesos."
Antike Welt 14.3 (1983):53-55.

423 _____. "Nymphaeum des C. Laekanius Bassus."
JÖAI 50 (1972-1975):Grabungen in Ephesos von 1960-
1969 bzw. 1970, 301-310.

424 Fossel-Peschl, Elisabeth A. Die Basilika am Staatsmarkt
in Ephesos. Graz: Selbstverlag, 1982.

Fournier, Paul. See no. 1136.

425 Fränkel, Max. "Eine Münze mit altionischer Aufschrift."
Archäologische Zeitung 37 (1879):27-30.

426 Franke, Peter R. Kleinasien zur Römerzeit. Griechisches
Leben im Spiegel der Münzen. Munich: Verlag C. H.
Beck, 1968.

427 Franke, Peter R., and Schmitt, Rüdiger. "PHANEOS-
PHANOS EMI SEMA." Chiron 4 (1974):1-4.

Frel, Jiri. See no. 1277.

428 Friedländer, Julius. "Die Erwerbungen des kgl. Münzkabinetts vom 1 Januar 1877- 31. März 1878." Zeitschrift für Numismatik 6 (1879):1-26.

429 Frova, Antonio. "La Statua di Artemide Efesia a 'Caesarea Maritima.'" Bollettino d'Arte 47 (1962): 305-13.

430 Fuchs, Werner. "Aus den Museumsnotizen einer Stipendiatenreise des Jahres 1954." Boreas 2 (1979):59-61.

431 Furtwängler, Andreas E. "Griechische Vieltypenprägung und Münzbeamte." Schweizerische numismatische Rundschau 61 (1982):5-29.

432- Fyfe, Theodore. "Some Aspects of Greek Architecture."
33   Journal of the Royal Institute of British Architects 21 (1914):489-96.

434 Gabriélovich. Ephèse ou Jérusalem. Tombeau de la Sainte Vierge. Paris: Librairie Religieuse H. Oudin, 1897.

435 _____. Le tombeau de la Sainte Vierge à Ephèse. Paris: Oudin, 1905.

436 _____. Le tombeau de la Sainte Vierge à Ephèse; réponse au R. P. Barnabe d'Alsace. O. F. M., Paris, 1905.

437 Gallina, Mario. "Appendice II, Epigrafi relative ai teatri." In Daria De Bernardi Ferrero. Teatri Classici in Asia Minore. Rome: "L'Erma" di Bretschneider, 1974, 4:212-28 (nos. 12-23).

438 Galvano. Albino. Artemis Efesia. Il significato del politeismo greco. Milan: Adelphi, 1967.

439 Garcia y Bellido, Antonio. "Das Artemision von Sagunt." Madrider Mitteilungen 4 (1963):87-98.

440 Gardner, Percy. "The Electrum Coin with Inscription."
     Archäologische Zeitung 37 (1879):184-86.

441 Gauer, Werner. "Die Gruppe der ephesischen Amazonen,
     ein Denkmal des Perserfriedens." In Tania. Fest-
     schrift für Roland Hempe. Edited by H. A. Cahn
     and E. Simon. Mainz: Verlag von Zaberg, 1980,
     pp. 201-26.

442 Gerasimov, Todor. "Zollplombe mit dem Namen der
     Stadt Ephesus in Kleinasien [In Bulgarian, abstract
     in German]." Bulletin de l'Institut archéologique
     bulgare 34 (1974):318-19.

443 Gerkan, Armin von. Das Theater von Priene.
     Munich: Verlag F. Schmidt, 1921, pp. 90-93.

444 Gerstinger, Hans. "Die Malereien und Mosaiken der
     Siebenschläferkatakombe in Ephesos." In Forschun-
     gen in Ephesos. vol. 4.2 Das Cömoeterium der
     Sieben Schläfer. Baden at Vienna: Rudolf M.
     Rohrer, 1937, pp. 212-22.

445 Ghidini Tortorelli, M. "A proposito dell'Artemis Efesia."
     Nuova Rivista Storica 56 (1972):440-52.

446 Gjerstad, Einar. "Studies in Archaic Greek Chronology,
     2. Ephesus." Annals of Archaeology and Anthro-
     pology 24 (1937):15-34.

447 Gottwald, Odo. "Zwei ephesische Beschlüsse mit
     Totenehrungen." Mitteilungen des Vereines klas-
     sischer Philologen in Wien 10 (1933):120-26.

448 Greenewalt, Crawford H. "Ephesian Ware." California
     Studies in Classical Antiquity 6 (1973):91-122.

449 Greenhalgh, Michael. "Pliny, Vitruvius, and the inter-
     pretation of ancient architecture." Gazette des
     Beaux-Arts 116 (1974):297-304.

450 Grégoire, Henri. "Epigraphie Chrétienne. I. Les
     inscriptions hérétiques d'Asie Mineure. II. Inscrip-
     tions d'Ephèse." Byzantion 1 (1924):695-716.

451 _____. "Miettes d'histoire byzantine (IVme-VIme
siècle)." In Anatolian Studies Presented to Sir
William Mitchell Ramsay. Edited by W. H. Buckler
and W. M. Calder. Manchester: Manchester University Press, 1923, pp. 151-64.

452 _____. Recueil des inscriptions grecques chrétiennes
d'Asie Mineure. Paris: Ernest Leroux, 1922.

453 Greifenhagen, Adolf. "Ein ostgriechisches Elfenbein."
Jahrbuch der Berliner Museen 7 (1965):125-56.

454 Gren, Erik. Kleinasien und der Ostbalkan in der
wirtschaftlichen Entwicklung der römischen Kaiserzeit. Uppsala Universitets Arsskrift, 9. Uppsala:
A. B. Lundequistska Bokhandeln, 1941.

455 Griechische Terracotten aus Tanagra und Ephesos im
Berliner Museum. Berlin: Verlag von Ernst Wasmuth,
1878.

456 Griffiths, John Gwyn. "Xenophon of Ephesus on Isis
and Alexandria." In Hommages à Maarten J. Vermaseren. Edited by M. B. de Boer and T. A.
Edridge. EPRO, 68. Leiden: E. J. Brill, 1978,
1:409-37.

457 Groag, Edmund. "Notizen zur Geschichte kleinasiatischer Familien." JÖAI 10 (1907):282-99.

458 Grolig, Hedy. "Ephesos: Stadt des siebenten
Weltwunders." Antike Welt 1.1 (1970):55.

459 Grose, Sidney W. Catalogue of the McClean Collection
of Greek Coins (Fitzwilliam Museum). Vol. 3. Asia
Minor, Farther Asia, Egypt, Africa. Cambridge:
Cambridge University Press, 1929.

460 Grotefend, C. L. "Ephesos." In Real-Encyclopädie
der classischen Alterthumswissenschaft. Edited by
A. Pauly. Stuttgart: Verlag der J. B. Metzler'-
schen Buchhandlung, 1844, 3:165-66.

461 Grueber, H. A. Coins of the Roman Republic in the

British Museum. Oxford: Oxford University Press, 1970.

462 Grund, Alfred. "Ephesus und Milet." Lotos 59 (1911): 203-13.

463 _____. "Vorläufiger Bericht über physiogeographische Untersuchungen im Deltagebiet des Kleinen Mäander bei Ajasoluk (Ephesus)." Sitzungsberichte der Akademie der Wissenschaften Wien (Mathematisch-naturwissenschaftliche Klasse) 115 (1906):241-62.

464 Grundmann, Walter. "Paulus in Ephesus." Helikon 4 (1964):46-82.

465 Gsänger, Hans. Ephesos. Mysterienstätten der Menschheit. Freiburg: Verlag Die Kommenden, 1959.

466 _____. Ephesos. Zentrum der Artemis-Mysterien. Schaffhausen: Novalis Verlag, 1974.

467 Gschnitzer, Fritz. "Ein senatorischer cursus honorum des 3. Jahrhunderts aus Ephesos." JÖAI 42 (1955): Beibl. 59-72.

Gschwantler, Kurt. See no. 1055.

468 Gschwind, Karl. Der ephesische Johannes und die Artemis Ephesia. Wanderungen im Raum des antiken und frühchristlichen Ephesus. Basel: Stiftung "Für Ephesus," 1965.

469 _____. Wiedererwachendes Ephesus. 3rd ed. Frühchristliche Türkei, 1. Basel: Stiftung "Für Ephesus," 1954.

470 Guattani, G. A. "Statua di Diana Efesia, di Ostia." Memorie enciclopediche romane sulle belle arti, antichità 5 (1809):1-7.

471 Gültekin, Hakki, and Baran, Musa. "Selçuk Tepesinde Bulunan Miken Mezari." Türk Arkeoloji Dergisi 13.2 (1964):122-27.

472 Gültekin, Hakki; Seze, Cevat; and Baran, Musa.
"Efeste St. Jean Basilikasi Kazi ve Restorayon
Çalişmalari." Türk Arkeoloji Dergisi 12.1 (1962):
49-52.

Guerrini, Lucia. See no. 1244.

473 Guhl, Ernst. Ephesiaca. Berlin: Frederick Nicolaus,
1843.

474 Guidi, I. "Testi orientali inediti sopra i Sette
Dormienti di Efeso publicati e tradotti." Memorie
della Reale Accademia dei Lincei 3rd ser. 12 (1883):
343-445.

475 Guyer, S. "Die Kirchen von Ephesos." Christliche
Kunst 31 (1934):283-88.

476 _____. "Zwei spätantike Grabmonumente Nordmeso-
potamiens und der älteste Märtyrergrab-Typus der
christlichen Kunst." In Aus fünf Jahrtausenden
morgenlandischer Kultur. Festschrift Max F. von
Oppenheim zum 70. Geburtstage. Berlin: E. F.
Weidner, 1933, pp. 148-56.

477 Guyonnaud, Joseph. S. Paul à Ephèse. Lahors: 1900.

478 Habicht, Christian. "New Evidence on the Province of
Asia." Journal of Roman Studies 65 (1975):64-91.

479 _____. "Zwei römische Senatoren aus Kleinasien. II.
Ti. Claudius Severus, der erste Konsul aus Ephesos."
ZPE 13 (1974):4-6.

480 Habicht, Georg. "Erwerbungen der Sammlungen München
1916-1917: Münzsammlung." Archäologischer Anzeiger
(1919):32-36.

481 Hackett, Horatio H. "Ephesus." In Dr. William Smith's
Dictionary of the Bible. Revised and edited by
H. B. Hackett. Boston: Houghton, Mifflin and
Company, 1888, 1:747-51.

482 Hahland, Walter. "Ebertöter Antinoos-Androklos. Eine ephesische Antinoos-Ehrung antoninischer Zeit." JÖAI 41 (1954):54-77.

483 _____. "Theotokos, eine Kolossalplastik aus der Zeit des 3. ephesischen Konzils." In Studies Presented to David Moore Robinson on his seventieth Birthday. Edited by G. E. Mylonas. Saint Louis: Washington University, 1951, 1:781-93.

484 Halfmann, Helmut. Die Senatoren aus dem östlichen Teil des Imperium Romanum bis zum Ende des 2. Jahrhunderts n. Chr. Hypomnemata. Untersuchungen zur Antike und zu ihrem Nachleben, 58. Göttingen: Vandenhoeck & Ruprecht, 1979.

_____. See. no. 17.

485 Hanfmann, George M. A. From Croesus to Constantine. The Cities of Western Asia Minor and Their Arts in Greek and Roman Times. Ann Arbor: University of Michigan Press, 1975.

486 _____. "A 'Hittite' Priest from Ephesus." AJA 66 (1962):1-4.

487 Hanfmann, George M. A., and Waldbaum, Jane C. "Kybebe and Artemis. Two Anatolian Goddesses at Sardis." Archaeology 22 (1969):264-69.

488 Harl, Friederike. "Reste eines archaistischen Reliefpinax aus Ephesus in Wien." Archäologischer Anzeiger 88 (1973):133-37.

489 Hauben, H. "On two Ephesian citizenship decrees from the Diadochian Period." ZPE 9 (1972):57-58.

490 Hauser, Friedrich. "Eine Vermuthung über die Bronzestatue aus Ephesos." JÖAI 5 (1902):214-16.

491 Head, Barclay V. "Apollo Hikesios." Journal of Hellenic Studies 10 (1889):43-45.

492 _____. Catalogue of the Greek Coins of Ionia. Catalogue of the Greek Coins in the British Museum. London: British Museum, 1892.

493 _____. "Coinage of Ephesus. Addenda et Corrigenda." Numismatic Chronicle 3rd ser. 1 (1881):13-23.

494 _____. "The Coins." In Excavations at Ephesus.
The Archaic Artemisia. Edited by D. G. Hogarth.
London: Longmans and Co., 1908, pp. 74-93.

495 _____. "Ephesian Tesserae." Numismatic Chronicle
4th ser. 8 (1908):281-86.

496 _____. Historia Numorum, A Manual of Greek Numismatics. 2nd ed. Oxford: Clarendon Press, 1911.

497 _____. On the Chronological Sequence of the Coins
of Ephesus. London: Rollin & Feuardent, 1880.

498 Heberdey, Rudolf. "Die Ausgrabungen in Ephesus in
den Jahren 1900 und 1901." Anz. Wien 39 (1902):
37-49.

499 _____. "Bericht über die ephesischen Grabungen im
Jahre 1904." Anz. Wien 42 (1905):81-97.

500 _____. "Daitis. Ein Beitrag zum ephesischen
Artemiscult." JÖAI 7 (1904):210-15.

501 _____. "Inschrift zu Ehren des Cn. Domitius Cor-
bulo." In Festheft der Wiener Studien Eugenio Bor-
mann zum 60. Geburtstag. Vienna: C. Gerhold's
Sohn, 1902, pp. 51-52 [=Wiener Studien, 24 (1902):
283-84].

502 _____. "Nachtrag zum ephesischen Berichte für
1902-1903." JÖAI 7 (1904):Beibl. 157-60.

503 _____. "Nikanor Aristotelous Stageirites." In
Festschrift Theodor Gomperz dargebracht zum
siebzigsten Geburtstage. Vienna: A. Hölder, 1902,
pp. 412-16.

504 _____. Das Theater (Inschriften) In Forschungen
in Ephesos. Vienna: Alfred Hölder, 1912, 2:95-203.

505 _____. "Vorläufige Berichte über die Ausgrabungen
in Ephesos, II." JÖAI 1 (1898):Beibl. 71-82.

506 _____. "Vorläufiger Bericht über die Ausgrabungen in Ephesus im Jahre 1899." Anz. Wien 37 (1900): 30-40.

507 _____. "Vorläufiger Bericht über die Ausgrabungen in Ephesus, III." JÖAI 2 (1899):Beibl. 37-50.

508 _____. "Vorläufiger Bericht über die Ausgrabungen in Ephesus, IV." JÖAI 3 (1900):Beibl. 83-96.

509 _____. "Vorläufiger Bericht über die Ausgrabungen in Ephesus, V." JÖAI 5 (1902):Beibl. 53-66.

510 _____. "Vorläufiger Bericht über die Grabungen in Ephesos 1902-3." Anz. Wien 41 (1904):50-67.

511 _____. "Vorläufiger Bericht über die Grabungen in Ephesus 1902-3, VI." JÖAI 7 (1904):Beibl. 37-56.

512 _____. "Vorläufiger Bericht über die Grabungen in Ephesus 1904, VII." JÖAI 8 (1905):Beibl. 61-80.

513 _____. "Vorläufiger Bericht über die Grabungen in Ephesus 1905-06, VIII." JÖAI 10 (1907):Beibl. 61-78.

514 _____. "Vorläufiger Bericht über die Grabungen in Ephesos 1907-1911, IX." JÖAI 15 (1912):Beibl. 157-82.

515 _____. "Vorläufiger Bericht über die Grabungen in Ephesos 1913, XI." JÖAI 18 (1915):Beibl. 77-88.

516 _____. "Zum Erlass des Kaisers Valens an Eutropius." JÖAI 9 (1906):182-92.

517 _____. "Zur Bibliothek in Ephesus." JÖAI 9 (1906): Beibl. 59.

518 _____. "Zur ephesischen Athletenbronze." JÖAI 19-20 (1919):247-52.

_____. See nos. 1036, 1498, 1499, 1501.

519 Heberdey, Rudolf; Wilberg, Wilhelm; and Niemann, George. Forschungen in Ephesos. vol. 2: Das

Theater in Ephesos. Vienna: Alfred Hölder, 1912.

520 Hegyi, Dolores. "Basileion ton Ionon." Acta antiqua Academiae scientiarum hungaricae 25 (1977):321-24.

521 Heinzel, Elma. "Zum Kult der Artemis von Ephesos." JÖAI 50 (1972-1973):243-51.

522 Hemer, Colin J. "Audeitorion." Tyndale Bulletin 24 (1973):128.

523 _____. The Letters to the Seven Churches of Asia in their Local Setting. Journal for the Study of the New Testament Supplement Series, 11. Sheffield: JSOT, 1986.

524 _____. "A Study of the Letters to the Seven Churches of Asia with Special Reference to Their Local Background." Dissertation, University of Manchester, 1969.

525 Henderson, Arthur E. "Excavations at Ephesus and Restoration of the Croesus (sixth century B.C.) structure." Journal of the Royal Institute of British Architects 16 (1909):538-40.

526 _____. "The Hellenistic Temple of Artemis at Ephesus." Journal of the Royal Institute of British Architects 22 (1915):130-34.

527 _____. "The Temple of Artemis (Diana) at Ephesus. Restoration of the Hellenistic (IV Century B.C.) Structure as it Appeared in the Time of St. Paul." Records of the Past 10 (1911):247-48.

528 _____. "The Temple of Diana at Ephesus." Journal of the Royal Institute of British Architects 41 (1933): 767-71.

_____. See nos. 568, 569.

528a Herold, Karl. "Restaurierung und Konservierung der Wandmalereien im Hanghaus 2, Ephesos." Anz. Wien 119 (1982):78-84.

529 Herrmann, Peter. "Cn. Domitius Ahenobarbus Patronus von Ephesos und Samos." ZPE 14 (1974):257-58.

530 _____. "Nochmals zu dem Brief Attalos' II. an die Ephesier." ZPE 22 (1976):233-34.

531 Hertzberg, Gustav. "Ephesus." In Handwörterbuch des biblischen Altertums für gebildete Bibelleser. Edited by E. Riehm. Leipzig: Verlag von Belhafen und Klafing, 1884, 1:383-86.

532 Herzog, Rudolf. "Ephesos und Milet." Klio 1 (1906): 529-32.

533 Hicks, Edward L. The Collection of Ancient Greek Inscriptions in the British Museum. Pt. 3, sec. 2. Oxford: Clarendon Press, 1890.

533a _____. "Demetrius the Silversmith. An Ephesian Study." Expositor 4th ser. 1 (1890):401-22.

534 _____. "Ephesus. A Postscript." Expositor 4th ser. 2 (1890):144-49.

535 Hild, J. A. "Ephesia." In Dictionnaire des antiquités grecques et romaines. Edited by C. Daremberg and E. Saglio. Graz: Akademische Druck- und Verlagsanstalt, 1963, 2:639.

536 Hill, George F. "Greek Coins Acquired by the British Museum, 1911-1912." Numismatic Chronicle 4th ser. 13 (1913):257-75.

537 _____. "Notes on Additions to the Greek Coins in the British Museum, 1887-1896." Journal of Hellenic Studies 17 (1897):78-91.

538 _____. "Priester-Diademe." JÖAI 2 (1899):245-49.

539 Hiller, Hilde. Ionische Grabreliefs der ersten Hälfte des 5. Jahrhunderts v. Chr. Istanbuler Mitteilungen, Beiheft 12. Tübingen: Verlag Ernst Wasmuth 1975. pp. 26-32.

540 Höfer, Otto. Mythologisch-Epigraphisches. Dresden: Druck von B. G. Teubner, 1910.

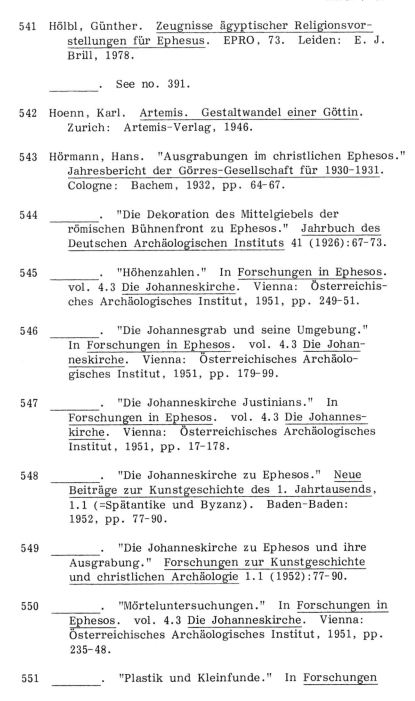

541 Hölbl, Günther. Zeugnisse ägyptischer Religionsvor-
stellungen für Ephesus. EPRO, 73. Leiden: E. J.
Brill, 1978.

_____. See no. 391.

542 Hoenn, Karl. Artemis. Gestaltwandel einer Göttin.
Zurich: Artemis-Verlag, 1946.

543 Hörmann, Hans. "Ausgrabungen im christlichen Ephesos."
Jahresbericht der Görres-Gesellschaft für 1930-1931.
Cologne: Bachem, 1932, pp. 64-67.

544 _____. "Die Dekoration des Mittelgiebels der
römischen Bühnenfront zu Ephesos." Jahrbuch des
Deutschen Archäologischen Instituts 41 (1926):67-73.

545 _____. "Höhenzahlen." In Forschungen in Ephesos.
vol. 4.3 Die Johanneskirche. Vienna: Österreichisches Archäologisches Institut, 1951, pp. 249-51.

546 _____. "Die Johannesgrab und seine Umgebung."
In Forschungen in Ephesos. vol. 4.3 Die Johanneskirche. Vienna: Österreichisches Archäologisches Institut, 1951, pp. 179-99.

547 _____. "Die Johanneskirche Justinians." In
Forschungen in Ephesos. vol. 4.3 Die Johannes-
kirche. Vienna: Österreichisches Archäologisches
Institut, 1951, pp. 17-178.

548 _____. "Die Johanneskirche zu Ephesos." Neue
Beiträge zur Kunstgeschichte des 1. Jahrtausends,
1.1 (=Spätantike und Byzanz). Baden-Baden:
1952, pp. 77-90.

549 _____. "Die Johanneskirche zu Ephesos und ihre
Ausgrabung." Forschungen zur Kunstgeschichte
und christlichen Archäologie 1.1 (1952):77-90.

550 _____. "Mörteluntersuchungen." In Forschungen in
Ephesos. vol. 4.3 Die Johanneskirche. Vienna:
Österreichisches Archäologisches Institut, 1951, pp.
235-48.

551 _____. "Plastik und Kleinfunde." In Forschungen

in Ephesos. vol. 4.3 Die Johanneskirche. Vienna: Österreichisches Archäologisches Institut, 1951, pp. 252-67.

552 _____. "Die römische Bühnenfront zu Ephesos." Jahrbuch des Deutschen Archäologischen Instituts 38-39 (1923-1924):275-345.

553 _____. "Stellung der Johanneskirche in der Entwicklung des byzantinischen Kirchenbaues." In Forschungen in Ephesos. vol. 4.3 Die Johanneskirche. Vienna: Österreichisches Archäologisches Institut, 1951, pp. 296-306.

554 _____. "Vorjustinianische Kirchenlage." In Forschungen in Ephesos. vol. 4.3 Die Johanneskirche. Vienna: Österreichisches Archäologisches Institut, 1951, pp. 200-234.

555 _____. "Das Westtor der Agora in Ephesos." JÖAI 25 (1929):22-53.

556 Hogarth, David G. "Bronze, Lead and Iron." In Excavations at Ephesus. The Archaic Artemisia. Edited by D. G. Hogarth. London: Longmans and Co., 1908, pp. 145-54.

557 _____. "Earlier Researches." In Excavations at Ephesus. The Archaic Artemisia. Edited by D. G. Hogarth. London: Longmans and Co., 1908, pp. 9-18.

558 _____. "Excavations of 1904-5." In Excavations at Ephesus. The Archaic Artemisia. Edited by D. G. Hogarth. London: Longmans and Co., 1908, pp. 19-51.

559 _____. "The Goddess." In Excavations at Ephesus. The Archaic Artemisia. Edited by D. G. Hogarth. London: Longmans and Co., 1908, pp. 323-38.

560 _____. "Gold and Electrum Jewellery." In Excavations at Ephesus. The Archaic Artemisia. Edited by D. G. Hogarth. London: Longmans and Co., 1908, pp. 94-115.

561 _____. "Literary Evidence." In Excavations at
Ephesus. The Archaic Artemisia. Edited by D. G.
Hogarth. London: Longmans and Co., 1908, pp.
1-8.

562 _____. "Other Ivory and Bone Objects." In Excavations at Ephesus. The Archaic Artemisia. Edited
by D. G. Hogarth. London: Longmans and Co.,
1908, pp. 186-98.

563 _____. "The Primitive Objects as a Whole." In
Excavations at Ephesus. The Archaic Artemisia.
Edited by D. G. Hogarth. London: Longmans and
Co., 1908, pp. 232-46.

564 _____. "Silver." In Excavations at Ephesus. The
Archaic Artemisia. Edited by D. G. Hogarth.
London: Longmans and Co., 1908, pp. 116-44.

565 _____. "Small Objects from the Croesus Temple."
In Excavations at Ephesus. The Archaic Artemisia.
Edited by D. G. Hogarth. London: Longmans and
Co., 1908, pp. 313-22.

566 _____. "Stone, Amber, Horn, Wood and Shell."
In Excavations at Ephesus. The Archaic Artemisia.
Edited by D. G. Hogarth. London: Longmans and
Co., 1908, pp. 210-17.

567 _____. "Terracotta, Glazed Ware, and Glass." In
Excavations at Ephesus. The Archaic Artemisia.
Edited by D. G. Hogarth. London: Longmans and
Co., 1908, pp. 199-209.

568 Hogarth, David G., and Henderson, Arthur E. "The
Croesus Structure. Temple D." In Excavations at
Ephesus. The Archaic Artemisia. Edited by D. G.
Hogarth. London: Longmans and Co., 1908, pp.
247-92.

569 _____. "The Primitive Structures." In Excavations
at Ephesus. The Archaic Artemisia. Edited by
D. G. Hogarth. London: Longmans and Co.,
1908, pp. 52-73.

570 Holleaux, Maurice. "Ephèse et les Priéniens 'du Charax.'" Revue études grecques 29 (1916):29-45.

571 Holtheide, B. "Eine Ehrenstatue für Claudia Dracontis (IK [Ephesos], 1562)." ZPE 45 (1982):97-99.

572 Hommel, Peter. "Giebel und Himmel." Istanbuler Mitteilungen 7 (1957):29-55.

573 Honigmann, Ernst. "Stephen of Ephesus and the Legend of the Seven Sleepers." Patristic Studies. Studi e Testi, 173. Vatican: Biblioteca Apostolica Vaticana, 1953, pp. 125-68.

574 Hopfgartner, Lois. "Die Entdeckung des spätbyzantinischen und genuesischen Ephesos." Studi genvensi 4 (1962-1963):17-81.

575 Horn, Rudolf. "Hellenistische Köpfe II, I. Weibliche Köpfe auf hellenistischen Münzen." Mitteilungen des Deutschen Archäologischen Instituts (Römische Abteilung) 53 (1938):70-77.

576 Hornblower, Simon. "Thucydides, the Panionian festival, and the Ephesia (III 104)." Historia 31 (1982): 241-45.

577 Howson, John S. "Ephesus." In Dr. William Smith's Dictionary of the Bible. Revised and edited by H. B. Hackett. Vol. 1:747-51. Boston: Houghton, Mifflin and Co., 1888.

_____. See no. 231.

578 Hueber, Friedmund J. "Antike Baudenkmäler als Aufgabengebiet des Architekten." In Lebendige Altertumswissenschaft. Festgabe zur Vollendung des 70. Lebensjahres von Hermann Vetters dargebracht von Freunden, Schülern und Kollegen. Vienna: Verlag Adolf Holzhausens Nfg., 1985, pp. 391-98.

579 _____. "Beobachtungen zu Kurvatur und Scheinperspektive an der Celsusbibliothek und anderen kaiserzeitlichen Bauten." Bauplanung und Bautheorie der Antike. Diskussionen zur archäologischen

Bauforschung, 4. Berlin: Deutsches Archäologisches Institut, 1983, pp. 175-200.

580   _____. "Bericht über die Wiederaufrichtungsarbeiten an der Celsusbibliothek, und über die bisherigen Ergebnisse der Untersuchungen der Bausubstanz." In The Proceedings of the Xth International Congress of Classical Archaeology. Edited by E. Akurgal. Ankara: Türk Tarih Kurumu Basimevi, 1978, 2:979-87.

581   _____. "Die Celsus-Bibliothek in Ephesos." Aspekte 2 (1978):Sondernummer.

582   _____. "Der Embolos, ein urbanes Zentrum von Ephesos." Antike Welt 15.4 (1984):1-23.

583   _____. "Theorie und Praxis der Anastylose und ihre Bedeutung für die Bauforschung." Dissertation, Technical University of Vienna, 1978.

584   _____. "Zur Anastylose des S-Tores der Agora in Ephesos." In Koldewey-Gesellschaft. Bericht über die 32 Tagung für Ausgrabungswissenschaft und Bauforschung. Innsbruck: 1984.

_____. See nos. 43, 1241, 1323, 1324.

585   Hueber, Friedmund J., and Strocka, Volker M. "Die Bibliothek des Celsus. Eine Prachtfassade in Ephesos und das Problem ihrer Wiederaufrichtung." Antike Welt 6.4 (1975):3-14.

586   Hultsch, Friedrick. Heraion und Artemision, zwei Tempelbauten Ioniens. Ein Vortrag. Berlin: Weidmannsche Buchhandlung, 1881.

587   Iacopi, G. "Efeso, capitale della provincia d'Asia." Vie del Mondo 10 (1942):363-76.

Içten, Cengiz. See no. 210.

588   Imhoof-Blumer, Friedrich. "Amazonen auf griechischen Münzen." Nomisma 2 (1908):1-18.

589 _____ . "Antike Münzbilder." Jahrbuch des
Deutschen Archäologischen Instituts 3 (1888):286-97.

589a _____ . "Beiträge zur Erklärung griechischer
Münztypen." Nomisma 6 (1911):1-23.

590 _____ . "Fluss-und Meergötter auf griechischen und
römischen Münzen." Revue suisse de numismatique
23 (1924):173-421.

591 _____ . "Griechische Münzen im königlichen Münz-
kabinett im Haag und in anderen Sammlungen."
Zeitschrift für Numismatik 3 (1876):269-353.

592 _____ . Griechische Münzen. Neue Beiträge und
Untersuchungen. Munich: Verlag der k. Akademie,
1890.

593 _____ . Kleinasiatische Münzen. Sonderschriften des
Österreichischen Archäologischen Institutes in Wien,
1. Vienna: Alfred Hölder, 1901-1902, 1:49-62;
2:513.

594 _____ . Zur griechischen und römischen Münzkunde.
Geneva: Verlag der Schweiz. Numism. Gesellschaft,
1908.

Inan, Jale. See no. 16.

595 Inan, Jale, and Alföldi-Rosenbaum, Elisabeth.
Römische und frühbyzantinische Porträtplastik aus
der Türkei. Neue Funde. Mainz: Zabern, 1979.

596 Inan, Jale, and Rosenbaum, Elisabeth. Roman and
Early Byzantine Portrait Sculpture in Asia Minor.
London: Oxford University Press, 1966.

597 Iplikçioğlu, [Sitki Isa] Bülent. "Prosopographisches
aus Ephesos." In Lebendige Altertumswissenschaft.
Festgabe zur Vollendung des 70. Lebensjahres von
Hermann Vetters dargebracht von Freunden, Schülern
und Kollegen. Vienna: Verlag Adolf Holzhausens Nfg.,
1985, pp. 135-37.

598 _____ . Die Repräsentanten des senatorischen

Reichsdienstes in Asia bis Diokletian im Spiegel der ephesischen Inschriften. Vienna: Verlag Verband der wissenschaftlichen Gesellschaften Österreichs, 1983.

_____. See nos. 766, 767, 768.

599 Işler, T. Ridvan. "Efes Müzesinde Konservasyon Çalişmalari." Efes Müzesi Yilliği 2 (1973-1978):80-82.

600 Jacobsthal, Paul. "The Date of the Ephesian Foundation-Deposit." Journal of Hellenic Studies 71 (1951): 85-95.

601 Janin, R. "Ephèse." In Dictionnaire d'histoire et de géographie ecclésiastiques. Edited by R. Aubert and E. van Cauwenbergh. Paris: Letouzey et Ané, 1963, 15:554-61.

602 Jenkins, G. K. "Recent acquisitions of Greek coins." British Museum Quarterly 27 (1963-1964):23-27.

603 Jentel, Marie-Odile. "Isis ou la Tyché d'Alexandrie?" In Hommages à Maarten J. Vermaseren. EPRO, 68. Leiden: E. J. Brill, 1978, 2:539-60.

604 Jessen. "Ephesia." In Paulys Realencyclopädie der classischen Altertumswissenschaft. Edited by G. Wissowa. Stuttgart: J. B. Metzlersche Buchhandlung, 1905, 5:2753-71.

605 Joannidis, Basileios. "Ephesus." In Biblisch-Historisches Handwörterbuch. Landeskunde, Geschichte, Religion, Kultur, Literatur. Edited by B. Reicke and L. Rost. Göttingen: Vandenhoeck and Ruprecht, 1962, 1:418-19.

606 Jobst, Werner. "Archäologische Denkmäler des Kaiserkults in Ephesos." In Aufstieg und Niedergang der römischen Welt. II 18.1: At Press.

607 _____. "Die Büsten im Weingartenmosaik von Santa Costanza." Mitteilungen des Deutschen Archäologischen Instituts (Römische Abteilung) 83 (1976):431-37.

608 _____. Corpus der antiken Mosaiken Kleinasiens.
I: Römische Mosaiken aus Ephesos. 1: Die
Hanghäuser des Embolos. Mit einem Beitr. von H.
Vetters. (=Forschungen in Ephesos. 8.2). Vienna:
Verlag der Österreichischen Akademie der Wissen-
schaften, 1977.

609 _____. "Griechische Wandinschriften aus dem Hanghaus II in Ephesos." Wiener Studien n.f. 6 (1972):
235-45.

610 _____. "Hellenistische Aussenfortifikationen um
Ephesos." In Studien zur Religion und Kultur
Kleinasiens. Festschrift für Friedrich Karl Dörner
zum 65. Geburtstag am 28. Februar 1976. Edited
by S. Şahin, E. Schwertheim, and J. Wagner.
EPRO, 66.1. Leiden: E. J. Brill, 1978, 1:447-56.

611 _____. "Ein Hospitium im Hanghaus 2 von Ephesos."
In Lebendige Altertumswissenschaft. Festgabe zur
Vollendung des 70. Lebensjahres von Hermann Vetters dargebracht von Freunden, Schülern und Kollegen. Vienna: Verlag Adolf Holzhausens Nfg., 1985,
pp. 200-203.

612 _____. "Das 'öffentliche Freudenhaus' in Ephesos."
JÖAI 51 (1976-1977):61-84.

613 _____. "Porträtkopf des Tiberius aus Ephesos." In
Forschungen und Funde-Festschrift Bernhard Neutsch.
Edited by F. Krinzinger, B. Otto, and E. Walde-
Psenner. Innsbrucker Beiträge zur Kulturwissenschaft,
21. Innsbruck: Institut für Sprachwissenschaft der
Universität Innsbruck, 1980, pp. 197-200.

614 _____. "Römische Mosaiken in Ephesos." In The
Proceedings of the Xth International Congress of
Classical Archaeology. Edited E. Akurgal. Ankara:
Türk Tarih Kurumu Basimevi, 1978, 2:653-60.

615 _____. "Untersuchungen an den römischen Mosaiken
von Ephesos." Efes Harabeleri ve Müzesi Yilliği 1
(1972):67-69.

616 _____. "1972 Yilinda Efes'te Roma Mozaikleri Üzerine

Yapilan Araştirmalar." Efes Harabeleri ve Müzesi Yilliği 1 (1972):65-66.

617 _____. "Zum Narthexmosaik der Marienkirche in Ephesos." JÖAI 49 (1968-1971):Beibl. 297-98.

618 _____. "Zum Standort der Partherdenkmales in Ephesos." In Koldewey-Gesellschaft. Bericht über die 32. Tagungsbericht. Innsbruck: 1984.

619 _____. "Zur Bau-und Bildkunst der Spätantike Ephesos." In Pro Arte Antiqua. Festschrift für Hedwig Kenner. 2: At Press. Sonderschriften herausgegeben vom Österreichischen Archäologischen Institut, 18. Vienna: Verlag A. F. Koska.

620 _____. "Zur Bestattungskirche der Sieben Schläfer in Ephesos." JÖAI 50 (1972-1975):Beibl. 171-80.

621 _____. "Zur Lokalisierung des Sebasteion-Augusteum in Ephesos." Istanbuler Mitteilungen 30 (1980):241-60.

622 _____. "Zur Standortbestimmung und Rekonstruktion des Parthersiegaltares von Ephesos." JÖAI 56 (1985): 79-82.

623 Jobst, Werner (mit einem Anhang [Fundbericht] von Christine Schwanzar). "Embolosforschungen I. Archäologische Untersuchungen östlich der Celsus-bibliothek in Ephesos." JÖAI 54 (1983):Beibl. 149-250.

624 Jobst, Werner, and Meriç, Recep. "Ein spätrömischer Mosaikboden in Pygela(?) [südlich von Ephesos]." JÖAI 52 (1978-1980):Beibl. 45-50.

Johnson, Allan C. See no. 1.

625 Johnson, David R. "The Library of Celsus, an Ephesian Phoenix." Wilson Library Bulletin 54 (1980):651-53.

625a Johnson, Lora L. "The Hellenistic and Roman Library: Studies Pertaining to Their Architectural Form." Dissertation, Brown University, 1984.

626 Johnson, Sherman E. "The Apostle Paul and the Riot
     in Ephesus." Lexington Theological Quarterly 14
     (October 1979):79-88.

627 Johnston, A. E. M. "The Earliest Preserved Greek
     Map: a New Ionian Coin Type." The Journal of
     Hellenic Studies 87 (1967):86-94.

628 Jones, Allen H. Essenes. The Elect of Israel and the
     Priests of Artemis. New York: University Press of
     America, 1985.

629 Jones, C. P. "A Deed of Foundation from the Terri-
     tory of Ephesos." Journal of Roman Studies 73
     (1983):116-25.

630 Jongh, E. D. J. de. "De tempel te Ephese en het
     beeld van Diana." Gereformeerd theologisch tijdschrift
     26 (1926):461-75.

631 Jordanides, Eustratios. "Ruines de la plaine du Caystre.
     I. L'aqueduc d'Ephèse." Revue des études anciennes
     7 (1905):221.

632 Kagan, Donald. "The Dates of the Earliest Coins."
     AJA 86 (1982):343-60.

633 Kahrstedt, Ulrich. "Frauen auf antiken Münzen." Klio
     10 (1910):261-314.

634 Kalinka, Ernst. "Das Palladas-Epigramm in Ephesos."
     In Festheft der Wiener Studien Eugenio Bormann zum
     60. Geburtstag. Vienna: C. Gerhold's Sonn, 1902,
     pp. 60-63. [=Wiener Studien 24 (1902):292-95].

635 Kandemir, S. The Antiquities of Ephesus. Izmir, n.d.

636 _____. Efes Harabeleri Rehberi. Izmir, n.d.

637 _____. Guide des ruines d'Ephèse. Izmir, n.d.

638 Kantorowicz, Ernst H. "Oriens Augusti-Lever du Roi."
     Dumbarton Oaks Papers 17 (1963):119-77.

Karabacek, Josef von. See no. 1037.

639 Karo, George. Greek Personality in Archaic Sculpture.
Martin Classical Lectures, 11. Cambridge, Harvard
University Press, 1948, pp. 216-20.

640 Karwiese, Stefan. "Archäologie und Numismatik."
Litterae Numismaticae Vindobonenses 2 (1983):281-97.

641 _____. "Attis in der antiken Kunst." Dissertation,
University of Vienna, 1967, pp. 208-13.

642 _____. "Das Beben unter Gallien and seine anhalten-
den Folgen." In Lebendige Altertumswissenschaft.
Festgabe zur Vollendung des 70. Lebensjahres von
Hermann Vetters dargebracht von Freunden, Schülern
und Kollegen. Vienna: Verlag Adolf Holzhausens
Nfg., 1985, pp. 126-131.

643 _____. "Der Caesar MAXIMUS und die Homonoia
AKMONEIA-EUMENEIA." Numismatische Zeitschrift
86 (1971):40-42.

644 _____. "Ephesos: C. Numismatischer Teil." Paulys
Realencyclopädie der classischen Altertumswissenschaft. Supplementband. Edited by K. Ziegler.
Stuttgart: Alfred Druckenmüller Verlag, 1970,
12:297-364.

645 _____. "Der gefesselte Attis." In Festschrift für
Fritz Eichler zum achtzigsten Geburtstag. Vienna:
Österreichisches Archäologisches Institut, 1967, pp.
82-95.

646 _____. "Koressos--Ein fast vergessener Stadtteil von
Ephesos." In Pro Arte Antiqua. Festschrift für
Hedwig Kenner. 2:214-25. Sonderschriften
herausgegeben vom Österreichischen Archäologischen
Institut, 18. Vienna: Verlag A. F. Koska.

647 _____. "Lysander as Herakliskos Drakonopnigon."
Numismatic Chronicle 7th ser. 20 (1980):1-27.

648 _____. "Der Numismatiker-Archäologe." JÖAI 56
(1985):99-108.

649 _____. "Der Tote Attis." JÖAI 49 (1968-1971):
50-62.

650 _____. "Türkei/Ephesos 1978-1981." JÖAI 53
(1981-1982):Grabungen 1-7.

651 Kasper, Sándor. "Belevi-Grabtumulus." JÖAI 47
(1964-1965):Grabungen 1966, 12-16.

652 _____. "Der Tumulus von Belevi." Archäologischer
Anzeiger 90 (1975):223-32.

653 _____. "Der Tumulus von Belevi (Grabungsbericht)."
JÖAI 51 (1976-1977):Beibl. 127-80.

654 _____. "Der Tumulus von Belevi. Grabungsbericht."
In The Proceedings of the Xth International Congress
of Classical Archaeology. Edited by E. Akurgal.
Ankara: Türk Tarih Kurumu Basimevi, 1978, 1:387-
98.

_____. See no. 342.

655 Kater-Sibbes, G. J. F. Preliminary Catalogue of Sarapis
Monuments. EPRO, 36. Leiden: E. J. Brill, 1973.

656 Kayan, Duygu. "1972 Yili Efes Büyük Tiyatro Kazisinda
Bulunan Trajik Masklar." Efes Harabeleri ve Müzesi
Yilliği 1 (1972):56-64.

656a Kearsley, Rosalinde. "The Archiereiai of Asia and the
Relationship of the Asiarch and Archiereus of Asia."
Greek, Roman and Byzantine Studies 27 (1986):At
Press.

657 Keil, Josef. "Ärzteinschriften aus Ephesos." JÖAI 8
(1905):128-38.

658 _____. "Antike und Christentum in Ephesos." In
Von der Antike zum Christentum, Festgabe für
Victor Schultze zum 80. Geburtstag. Stettin: Verlag
Fischer and Schmidt, 1931, pp. 97-102.

659 _____. "Aphrodite Daitis." JÖAI 17 (1914):145-47.

660 _____. "Archäologische Funde/Anatolien."
Archäologischer Anzeiger (1930):444-62.

661 _____. "Artemis als Göttermutter und Himmelsköni-
gin." Charisma. Festgabe zur 25 jährigen Stiftungs-
feier des Vereines klassischer Philologen in Wien.
Vienna: Universität Wien, 1924, pp. 20-27.

662 _____. "Ausgrabungen in Ephesos." Klio 22 (1928):
161-62.

663 _____. "Die Ausgrabungen in Ephesos." Wiener
Blätter für die Freunde der Antike 5 (1928):50-53.

664 _____. "Die Ausgrabungen in Ephesos." Forschungen
und Fortschritte 4 (1928):7; 61-62.

665 _____. "Die Ausgrabungen in Ephesos." Forschungen
und Fortschritte 5 (1929):61.

666 _____. "Die Ausgrabungen in Ephesos." Forschungen
und Fortschritte 7 (1931):65-66.

667 _____. "Die Ausgrabungen in Ephesos." Forschungen
und Fortschritte 10 (1934):254-56.

668 _____. "Bericht über seine im April 1953 ausgeführte
Reise in die Türkei." Anz. Wien 90 (1953):141-42.

669 _____. "Eine Biologeninschrift aus Ephesos." Anz.
Wien 82 (1945):10-18.

670 _____. "Bürgerrechtdekret aus Pygela." JÖAI 23
(1926):Beibl. 73-90.

671 _____. "Denkmäler des Meter-Kultes." JÖAI 18
(1915):66-78.

672 _____. "Denkmäler des Sarapiskultes in Ephesos."
Anz. Wien 91 (1954):217-28.

673 _____. "Drei neue Inschriften aus Ephesos." JÖAI
35 (1943):Beibl. 101-108.

674 _____. "Die dritte Neokorie von Ephesos." Numismatische Zeitschrift 48 (1915):125-30.

675 _____. "Ephesische Bürgerrechts- und Proxeniedek-
rete aus dem vierten und dritten Jahrhundert v.
Chr." JÖAI 16 (1913):231-44.

676 _____. "Ephesische Funde und Beobachtungen."
JÖAI 18 (1915):Beibl. 279-86.

677 _____. "Die ephesischen Chiliastyen." JÖAI 16
(1913):245-48.

678 _____. "Ein ephesischer Anwalt des 3. Jahrhunderts
durchreist das Imperium Romanum." Sitzungsberichte,
Bayerische Akademie der Wissenschaften
(Philosophisch-historische Klasse) 3 (1956):3-10.

679 _____. "Ephesos." In Neue Deutsche Ausgrabungen.
Edited by G. Rodenwaldt. Deutschtum und Ausland,
23-24. Münster: Aschendorffsche Verlagsbuchhandlung, 1930, pp. 69-77.

680 _____. "Ephesos." Oriens Christianus 28 (1931):
1-14.

681 _____. Ephesos. Ein Führer durch die Ruinenstätte
und ihre Geschichte. Vienna: Hölder, 1915.

682 _____. Ephesos. Ein Führer durch die Ruinenstätte
und ihre Geschichte. 2nd ed. Augsburg: B.
Filser, 1932.

683 _____. Ephesos. Ein Führer durch die Ruinenstätte
und ihre Geschichte. 3rd ed. Vienna: Österreichisches Archäologisches Institut, 1955.

684 _____. Ephesos. Ein Führer durch die Ruinenstätte
und ihre Geschichte. 4th ed. Vienna: Österreichisches Archäologisches Institut, 1957.

685 _____. Ephesos. Ein Führer durch die Ruinenstätte
und ihre Geschichte. 5th ed. Vienna: Österreichisches Archäologisches Institut, 1964.

686 _____. "Ephesos und der Etappendienst zwischen der
Nord- und Ostfront des Imperium Romanum." Anz.
Wien 92 (1955):159-70.

687 _____. "Erlass des Prokonsuls L. ANTONIUS ALBUS über die Freihaltung des ephesischen Hafens." JÖAI 44 (1959):142-47.

688 _____. "Die erste Kaiserneokorie von Ephesos." Numismatische Zeitschrift 52 (1919):115-20.

689 _____. "Las excavaciones en Efeso." Investigacion y Progresso 5 (1931):49-50.

690 _____. "Die Familie des Prätorianerpräfekten Anthemius." Anz. Wien 79 (1942):185-203.

691 _____. "Geschichte der Ausgrabung." In Forschungen in Ephesos. vol. 4.3 Die Johanneskirche. Vienna: Österreichisches Archäologisches Institut, 1951, pp. 15-16.

692 _____. "Grabbau mit Unterweltsarkophag aus Ephesos." JÖAI 17 (1914):133-44.

693 _____. "Der Grabherr des Mausoleums von Belevi." Anz. Wien 86 (1949):51-60.

694 _____. "Inschrift aus Notion in Ephesos." JÖAI 15 (1912):67.

695 _____. "Inschriften." In Forschungen in Ephesos, vol. 4.1 Die Marienkirche in Ephesos. Vienna: Benno Filser, 1932, pp. 79-106.

696 _____. "Inschriften." In Forschungen in Ephesos. vol. 4.3 Die Johanneskirche. Vienna: Österreichisches Archäologisches Institut, 1951, pp. 275-95.

696a _____. "Die Inschriften von Ephesos und die Tituli Asiae Minoris." In Actes du dieuxieme congres international d'epigraphie grecque et latine (1952). Paris: Librairie d'amerique et d'orient Adrien Maisonneuve, 1953, pp. 202-09.

697 _____. "Die Iuventus von Virunum und die ephesische Ephebie." In Festschrift für Rudolf Egger. Beiträge zur älteren Europäischen Kultur Geschichte.

Klagenfurt: Verlag des Geschichtsvereins für
Kärnten, 1953, 2:261-64.

698 _____. "Johannes von Ephesos und Polykarpos von
Smyrna." In Strena Buliciana. Commentationes
gratulatoriae. Francisco Bulić. Zagreb: 1924:
pp. 367-72.

699 _____. "Kaiser Marcus und die Thronfolge." Klio
31 (1938):293-300.

700 _____. "Kulte im Prytaneion von Ephesos." In
Anatolian Studies Presented to William Hepburn
Buckler. Edited by W. M. Calder and J. Keil.
Manchester: University Press, 1939, pp. 119-28.

701 _____. "Die Lage des ephesischen 'Smyrna.'" JÖAI
31 (1938-1939):33-35.

702 _____. "Lydia (historischer Teil)." In Paulys Real-
encyclopädie der classischen Altertumswissenschaft.
Edited by W. Kroll. Stuttgart: J. B. Metzlersche
Verlagsbuchhandlung, 1927, 13.2:2161-2202.

703 _____. "Metropolis (no. 8)." Paulys Realencyclopädie der classischen Altertumswissenschaft. Edited
by W. Kroll. Stuttgart: J. B. Metzlerscher Verlag,
1932, 15:1497.

704 _____. "Eine neue Inschrift des C. Rutilius Gallicus
aus Ephesos." JÖAI 17 (1914):194-99.

705 _____. "Die neuen Ausgrabungen in Ephesos."
Archäologisches Institut des Deutschen Reiches.
Bericht über die Hundertjahrfeier 21-25 April 1929.
Berlin: Walter de Gruyter, 1930, pp. 225-27.

706 _____. "Die neuen Ausgrabungen in Ephesos."
Wiener Blätter für die Freunde der Antike 7 (1930):
35-37.

707 _____. "Ein Orakel des klarischen Apollon." Anz.
Wien 82 (1945):47-53.

708 _____. "Ortygia, die Geburtsstätte der ephesischen
Artemis." JÖAI 21-22 (1922-1924):113-19.

709 _____. "Ein rätselhaftes Amulett." JÖAI 32 (1940): 79-84.

710 _____. "Das Serapeion von Ephesos." In Bericht über den VI. Internationalen Kongress für Archäologie (Berlin 21.-26. August 1939). Edited by M. Wegner. Berlin: Walter de Gruyter & Co., 1940, p. 473.

711 _____. "Das Serapeion von Ephesos." In Halil Edhem Hatira Kitabi, Cilt:1 (=In Memoriam Halil Edhem, vol. 1). Türk Tarih Kurumu Yayinlarindar 7, Seri No. 5. Ankara: Türk Tarih Kurumu Basimevi, 1947, pp. 181-92.

712 _____. "Skulpturengruppen in Ephesos." JÖAI 39 (1952):42-46.

713 _____. "Das Unterrichtswesen im antiken Ephesos." Anz. Wien 88 (1951):331-36.

714 _____. "Die Vertreter der zweiten Sophistik in Ephesos." Anz. Wien 89 (1952):367-68.

715 _____. "Vertreter der zweiten Sophistik in Ephesos." JÖAI 40 (1953):5-26.

716 _____. "X. Vorläufiger Bericht über die Arbeiten in Ephesos 1912." JÖAI 15 (1912):Beibl. 183-212.

717 _____. "XII. Vorläufiger Bericht über die Ausgrabungen in Ephesos." JÖAI 23 (1926):Beibl. 247-300.

718 _____. "XIII. Vorläufiger Bericht über die Ausgrabungen in Ephesos." JÖAI 24 (1929):Beibl. 5-68.

719 _____. "XIV. Vorläufiger Bericht über die Ausgrabungen in Ephesos." JÖAI 25 (1929):Beibl. 5-52.

720 _____. "XV. Vorläufiger Bericht über die Ausgrabungen in Ephesos." JÖAI 26 (1930):Beibl. 5-66.

721 _____. "XVI. Vorläufiger Bericht über die Ausgrabungen in Ephesos." JÖAI 27 (1932):Beibl. 5-72.

722 _____. "XVII. Vorläufiger Bericht über die Ausgrabungen in Ephesos." JÖAI 28 (1933):Beibl. 5-44.

723 _____. "XVIII. Vorläufiger Bericht über die Ausgrabungen in Ephesos." JÖAI 29 (1935):Beibl. 103-
52.

724 _____. "XIX. Vorläufiger Bericht über die Ausgrabungen in Ephesos." JÖAI 30 (1937):Beibl. 173-
214.

725 _____. "Zum Martyrium des heiligen Timotheus in
Ephesos." JÖAI 29 (1935):82-92.

726 _____. "Zur ephesischen essenia." JÖAI 36
(1946):Beibl. 13-14.

727 _____. "Zur Geschichte der Hymnoden in der Provinz
Asia." JÖAI 11 (1908):101-110.

728 _____. "Zur Topographie der ionischen Küste
südlich von Ephesos." JÖAI 11 (1908):Beibl. 135-68.

729 _____. "Zur Topographie und Geschichte von
Ephesos." JÖAI 21-22 (1922-1924):96-112.

730 _____. "Die zwei Lebenswege in einem ephesischen
Epigramm." Serta Kazaroviniana. Commentationes
Gratulatioriae Gabrielo Kazarov. vol. 1:213-17.
[=Bulletin de l'Institut archéologique bulgare, 16
(1950):213-17].

_____. See nos. 1500, 1502.

731 Keil, Josef, and Maresch, Gustav. "Epigraphische
Nachlese zu Miltners Ausgrabungsberichten aus
Ephesos." JÖAI 45 (1960):Beibl. 75-100.

732 Kenner, Fr. "Stater von Ephesos." Numismatische
Zeitschrift 5 (1873):26-32.

733 Kienast, Dietmar. "Die Homonoiaverträge in der
römischen Zeit." Jahrbuch für Numismatik und
Geldgeschichte 14 (1964-1965):51-64.

734 _____. "Ionien." Jahrbuch für Numismatik und
Geldgeschichte 12 (1962):117-98.

735 _____. "Literaturüberblicke der griechischen
Numismatik: Cistophoren." Jahrbuch für Numismatik und Geldgeschichte 11 (1961):159-88.

736 Kirsten, Ernst. "Artemis von Ephesos und Eleuthera
von Myra mit Seitenblicken auf St. Nicolaus und auf
Kommagene." In Studien zur Religion und Kultur
Kleinasiens. Festschrift für Friedrich Karl Dörner
zum 65. Geburtstag am 28. Februar 1976. Edited
by S. Şahin, E. Schwertheim, and J. Wagner. EPRO,
66.2. Leiden: E. J. Brill, 1978, 2:457-88.

737 Kiss, A. "Deux chapiteaux romains de l'époque impériale."
Bulletin du Musée Hongrois des Beaux-Arts 30
(1967):7-17.

738 Klauser, Theodor. "Gottesgebärerin." In Reallexikon
für Antike und Christentum. Edited by Th. Klauser
et al. Stuttgart: Anton Hiersemann, 1981, 11:1071-
1103.

739 Kleiner, Fred S. "The Dates Cistophori of Ephesus."
American Numismatic Society Museum Notes 18 (1972):
17-32.

740 _____. "The Giresun Hoard." American Numismatic
Society Museum Notes 19 (1974):3-26.

741 Kleiner, Fred S., and Noe, Sydney P. The Early
Cistophoric Coinage. Numismatic Studies, 14. New
York: American Numismatic Society, 1977.

742 Kleiner, Gerhard. "Diadochen-Gräber." Sitzungsberichte der wissenschaftlichen Gesellschaft an der
Johann Wolfgang Goethe-Universität 1 (1963):67-85.

743 _____. "Hellenistische Sarkophage in Kleinasien."
Istanbuler Mitteilungen 7 (1957):1-10.

744 Knibbe, Dieter. "Der Asiarch M. Fulvius Publicianus
Nikephoros, die ephesischen Handwerkszünfte und

die Stoa des Servilius." JÖAI 56 (1985):71-
77.

745 _____. "Ephesos: A. Historisch-epigraphischer
Teil." Paulys Realencyclopädie der classischen
Altertumswissenschaft. Supplementband. Edited
by K. Ziegler. Stuttgart: Alfred Druckenmüller
Verlag, 1970, 12:248-97.

746 _____. "Ephesos nicht nur die Stadt der Artemis.
Die 'anderen' ephesischen Götter." In Studien zur
Religion und Kultur Kleinasiens. Festschrift für
Friedrich Karl Dörner zum 65. Geburtstag am 28.
Februar 1976. Edited by S. Şahin, E. Schwertheim,
and J. Wagner. EPRO, 66.2. Leiden: E. J. Brill,
1978, 2:489-503.

747 _____. "Epigraphische Nachlese im Bereiche der
ephesischen Agora." JÖAI 47 (1964-1965):Beibl.
1-44.

748 _____. Forschungen in Ephesos. 9.1.1. Der
Staatsmarkt. Die Inschriften des Prytaneions. Die
Kureteninschriften und sonstige religiöse Texte.
Vienna: Verlag der Österreichischen Akademie der
Wissenschaften, 1981.

749 _____. "Die Inschriften 1960-69." JÖAI 50 (1972-
1975):Grabungen in Ephesos von 1960-1969 bzw.
1970, 407-20.

750 _____. "Kaiserkult in Kleinasien." In Aufstieg und
Niedergang der römischen Welt. II 18.1: At press.

751 _____. "Neue ephesische Chiliastyen." JÖAI 46
(1961-1963):Beibl. 19-32.

752 _____. "Neue Inschriften aus Ephesos I." JÖAI 48
(1966-1967):Beibl. 1-22.

753 _____. "Neue Inschriften aus Ephesos II." JÖAI 49
(1968-1971):Beibl. 1-56.

754 _____. "Neue Inschriften aus Ephesos III." JÖAI
49 (1968-1971):Beibl. 57-88.

755 _____. "Neue Inschriften aus Ephesos IV." JÖAI
50 (1972-1975):Beibl. 1-26.

756 _____. "Neue Inschriften aus Ephesos V." JÖAI 50
(1972-1975):Beibl. 27-56.

757 _____. "Neue Inschriften aus Ephesos VI." JÖAI
50 (1972-1975):Beibl. 57-66.

758 _____. "Neue Inschriften aus Ephesos VII." JÖAI
50 (1972-1975):Beibl. 67-80.

759 _____. "Eine neue Kuretenliste aus Ephesos." JÖAI
54 (1938):125-27.

760 _____. "Die österreichischen Ausgrabungen und
Arbeiten in Ephesos und Belevi 1971 bis 1977."
Archiv für Orientforschung 26 (1978-1979):214-16.

761 _____. "Quandocumque quis trium virorum rei
publicae constituendae ... Ein neuer Text aus
Ephesos." ZPE 44 (1981):1-10.

762 _____. "Ein religiöser Frevel und seine Sühne. Ein
Todesurteil hellenistischer Zeit aus Ephesos." JÖAI
46 (1961-1963):175-82.

763 _____. "Tyche und das Kreuz Christi als antithe-
tische Bezugspunkte menschlichen Lebens in einer
frühchristlichen Inschrift aus Ephesos." In
Festschrift für Fritz Eichler zum achtzigsten
Geburtstag. Vienna: Österreichisches Archäologisches Institut, 1967, pp. 96-102.

_____. See nos. 44, 132, 361, 362, 363, 1453.

764 Knibbe, Dieter, and Alzinger, Wilhelm. "Ephesos vom
Beginn der römischen Herrschaft in Kleinasien bis
zum Ende der Principatszeit." In Aufstieg und
Niedergang der römischen Welt. Edited by H.
Temporini and W. Haase. Berlin: Walter de
Gruyter, 1980, II.7.2:748-830.

765 Knibbe, Dieter, and Engelmann, Helmut. "Neue
Inschriften aus Ephesos X." JÖAI 55 (1984):137-49.

766 Knibbe, Dieter, and Iplikçioğlu, Bülent. "Neue
Inschriften aus Ephesos VIII." JÖAI 53 (1981-1982):
87-150.

767 _____. "Neue Inschriften aus Ephesos IX." JÖAI 55
(1984):107-135.

768 Knibbe, Dieter, and Iplikçioğlu, Bülent (Mit Beiträgen
... von Friedel Schindler). Ephesos im Spiegel
seiner Inschriften. Vienna: Schindler, 1984.

769 Knibbe, Dieter; Meriç, Recep; and Merkelbach, Reinhold. "Der Grundbesitz der ephesischen Artemis im
Kaystrostal." ZPE 33 (1979):139-47.

770 Knibbe, Dieter, and Merkelbach, Reinhold. "Aller-
höchste Schelte (Zwei Exemplare der Sacrae Litterae
aus Ephesos)." ZPE 31 (1978):229-32.

771 _____. "Ephesische Bauinschriften 1. Der Strassen-
brunnen." ZPE 31 (1978):80.

772 _____. "Ephesische Bauinschriften 2. Die Inschrift
des Hydreions." ZPE 31 (1978):96-98.

773 _____. "Ephesische Bauinschriften 3. Das Varius-
bad." ZPE 31 (1978):99.

774 _____. "Ephesische Bauinschriften 4. Die Johanneskirche." ZPE 31 (1978):114.

775 _____. "Der ephesische grammateus tou demou M.
Tigellius Lupus." ZPE 33 (1979):124-25.

776 _____. "Grabepigramm aus Ephesos." ZPE 21 (1976):
191-92.

777 _____. "Togokleopatra." ZPE 34 (1979):238-39.

778 Knibbe, Dieter, and Vetters, Hermann. "Ephesos 1975-
1977." JÖAI 52 (1978-1980):Grabungen 1975-1977,
16-19.

779 Knoll, Fritz. "Baubeschreibung." In Forschungen in
Ephesos. vol. 4.1 Die Marienkirche in Ephesos.
Vienna: Benno Filser, 1932, pp. 13-78.

780 Koch, Herbert. "Die angebliche Skopas-Säule vom Jüngeren Artemision zu Ephesos." In Theoria, Festschrift für W. H. Schuchhardt. Baden-Baden: 1960, pp. 122-27.

781 Koenigs, Wolf, and Radt, Wolfgang. "Ein kaiserzeitlicher Rundbau (Monopteros) in Pergamon." Istanbuler Mitteilungen 29 (1979):317-54.

782 Kötting, Bernhard. Peregrinatio religiosa, Wallfahrten in der Antike und das Pilgerwesen in der alten Kirche. 2nd ed. Forschungen zur Volkskunde, 33.5. Munster: Th. Stenderhoff, 1980.

783 Kolendo, Jerzy. "Studia z dziejów numizmatyki. Zbiory w Krzemieńcu [article in Polish, summary in Russian and French]." Archeologia 20 (1969):92-106.

784 Kollwitz, Johannes. Oströmische Plastik der theodosianischen Zeit. Studien zur spätantiken Kunstgeschichte, 12. Berlin: Verlag von Walter de Gruyter, 1941, pp. 85-89.

785 Kopp, Clemens. "Das Mariengrab in Ephesus?" Theologie und Glaube 45 (1955):161-88.

786 Korzeniewski, Dietmar. "Trinkspruch auf eine grosszügige Gastgeberin." Gymnasium 81 (1974):513-19.

787 Koşay, Hamit, and Bilgi, Önder. "Excavations in Turkey in 1970 and 1971." Bulletin d'Archéologie Sud-Est Européenne 3 (1975):147-68.

788 Kosnetter, J. "100 Jahre Ausgrabungen in Ephesos." Die Zeit im Buch 17 (1963):30-32.

789 Kourouniotes, Konstantinos. "To ergon tes Hellenikes Archaiologikes Hyperesias en Mikra Asia." Deltion 7 (1921-1922):1-6.

790 Kraabel, Alf T. "Judaism in Western Asia Minor under the Roman Empire, with a Preliminary Study of the Jewish Community at Sardis, Lydia." Dissertation, Harvard Divinity School, 1968.

791 Kraft, Konrad. Das System der kaiserzeitlichen

Münzprägung in Kleinasien. Istanbuler Forschungen, 29. Berlin: Gebr. Mann Verlag, 1972.

792 Kraus, Theodor. Hekate. Studien zu Wesen und Bild der Göttin in Kleinasien und Griechenland. Heidelberger Kunstgeschichtliche Abhandlungen, n.f. 5. Heidelberg: Carl Winter Universitätsverlag, 1960, pp. 24-56.

793 Krause-Zimmer, Hella. Artemis Ephesia. Anregungen zur anthroposophischen Arbeit, 5. Stuttgart: Verlag Freies Geistesleben, 1964.

794 Krischen, Fritz. "Das Artemision von Ephesos." Wilhelm Dörpfeld Festschrift zum 80. Geburtstag. Edited by G. Martiny. Berlin: Verlag für Kunstwissenschaft, 1933, pp. 71-77.

795 _____. Weltwunder der Baukunst in Babylonien und Jonien. Tübingen: E. Wasmuth, 1956.

796 Kuhn, Gerhard. "Der Altar der Artemis in Ephesos." Mitteilungen des Deutschen Archäologischen Instituts (Athenische Abteilung) 99 (1984):199-216.

797 Kuhnert. "Ephesia Grammata." Paulys Realencyclopädie der classischen Altertumswissenschaft. Edited by G. Wissowa. Stuttgart: J. B. Metzlersche Verlagsbuchhandlung, 1905, 5.2:2771-73.

798 Kukula, Richard C. "Die angebliche Jahrtausendfeier des Dianatempels von Ephesus." Zeitschrift für die Österreichischen Gymnasien 1 (1904):1-7.

799 _____. "Brände des ephesischen Artemisions." JÖAI 8 (1905):Beibl. 23-32.

800 _____. "Inschriftliche Zeugnisse über das Artemision." In Forschungen in Ephesos. Vienna: Alfred Hölder, 1906, 1:278-82.

801 _____. "Literarische Zeugnisse über den Artemistempel." In Forschungen in Ephesos. Vienna: Alfred Hölder, 1906, 1:237-77.

802 Lacroix, Leon. "Quelques groupes de statues sur les monnaies de Corinthe." Revue archéologique 31-32 (1948):533-43.

803 _____. Les reproductions de statues sur les monnaies grecques. La statuaire archaïque et classique. Bibliothèque de la Faculté de Philosophie et Lettres de l'Université de Liège, 116. Liège: Faculté de philosophie et lettres, 1949.

804 Lähnemann, Johannes. "Die sieben Sendschreiben der Johannes-Apokalypse. Dokumente für die Konfrontation des frühen Christentums mit hellenistisch-römischer Kultur und Religion in Kleinasien." In Studien zur Religion und Kultur Kleinasiens. Festschrift für Friedrich Karl Dörner zum 65. Geburtstag am 28. Februar 1976. Edited by S. Şahin, E. Schwertheim, and J. Wagner. EPRO 66.2. Leiden: E. J. Brill, 1978, 2:516-39.

805 Lämmer, Manfred. Olympien und Hadrianeen im antiken Ephesos. Cologne: Universität Köln, 1967.

806 Lafaye, M. G. "Ephèse romaine. (les fouilles de 1896 à 1904)." Conférences faites au Musée Guimet. Annales de Musée Guimet. Bibliothèque de vulgarisation, 32. Paris: Ernest Leroux, 1909, pp. 1-44.

807 Lampakes, Georgios. Hoi hepta asteres tes Apokalypseos, etoi istoria, perisothenta ereipia, mnemeia kai nyn katastasis ton 7 ekklesion tes Asias Ephesou, Smyrnes, Pergamou, Thyateiron, Sardeon, Philadelphias kai Laodikeias, par' he Kolossai kai Hierapolis. Athens: Typois "Kratous" Th. Tzavella, 1909.

808 Lang, Gerhard J. "Zur oberen Osthalle der Agora, der 'Neronischen Halle' in Ephesos." In Lebendige Altertumswissenschaft. Festgabe zur Vollendung des 70. Lebensjahres von Hermann Vetters dargebracht von Freuden, Schülern und Kollegen. Vienna: Verlag Adolf Holzhausens Nfg., 1985, pp. 176-80.

809 _____. "Ein Zwischenbericht zur Anastylose des

Südtores der Agora von Ephesos." Antike Welt 15.4 (1984):23-30.

810 Langmann, Gerhard. "Ephesos, du Leuchte Asiens. Ein Rundblick." Antike Welt 10.4 (1979):3-20.

811 _____. "Eine Kaisertaufe (?) in Ephesos." JÖAI 56 (1985):65-69.

812 _____. "Seit 1895 Österreicher in Ephesos." Antike Welt 1.2 (1970):55.

813 _____. "Eine spätarchaische Nekropole unter dem Staatsmarkt zu Ephesos." In Festschrift für Fritz Eichler zum achtzigsten Geburtstag. Vienna: Österreichisches Archäologisches Institut, 1967, pp. 103-23.

814 _____. "Vom Aufstieg und Fall einer Weltstadt." In Türkei. 5.38 (n.d.):40-43.

815 _____. "Ein Zauberamulett aus Ephesos." Jahrbuch der Österreichischen Byzantinistik 22 (1973):281-84.

816 _____. "Ein Zauberamulett aus Ephesos." Antike Welt 9.3 (1978):60-61.

_____. See nos. 391, 422, 423.

817 Larsen, S. "The seven Churches in Asia Minor." Near East Service Quarterly 1 (October 1940):5-7.

818 Latte, Kurt. "Aphrodite in Ephesos." Archiv für Religionswissenschaft 17 (1914):678-79.

819 Lattimore, Steven. "The Bronze Apoxyomenos from Ephesos." AJA 76 (1972):13-16.

820 Laum, Bernhard. Stiftungen in der griechischen und römischen Antike. Leipzig: B. G. Teubner, 1914, 1:82-9.

821 Laurenzi, Luciano. "Le scuole artistiche di scultura dell'Asia Minore." Corsi di cultura ravennate e bizantina 12 (1965):375-404.

822 Lauria, Giuseppe Aurelio. Efeso; studj. Napoli, 1874.

823 Lauter, Hans. "Ein republikanisches Triumphalmonument aus Ephesos." In The Proceedings of the Xth International Congress of Classical Archaeology. Edited by E. Akurgal. Ankara: Türk Tarih Kurumu Basimevi, 1978, 2:925-31.

824 Lawson, A. J. "Unpublished Coins of Ephesus." Numismatic Chronicle 3rd ser. 2 (1882):351.

825 Le Bas, Philippe, and Waddington, William H. Voyage archéologique en Grèce et en Asie Mineure. Explication des inscriptions grecques et latines. Paris: Firmin-Didot, 1847-1877?.

826 Le Camus, Emile. "Ephèse." In Dictionnaire de la Bible. Edited by F. Vigouroux. Paris: Letouzey et Ané, 1899, 2:1831-49.

827 _____. Voyage aux sept Eglises de l'Apocalypse. Paris: Sanard et Derangeon, 1896.

828 Leclercq, Henri. "Ephèse." In Dictionnaire d'Archéologie chrétienne et de Liturgie. Edited by F. Cabrol and H. Leclercq. Paris: Librairie Letouzey et Ané, 1922, 5.1:118-42.

829 _____. "Sept dormants d'Ephèse." In Dictionnaire d'Archéologie chrétienne et de Liturgie. Edited by F. Cabrol and H. Leclercq. Paris: Librairie Letouzey et Ané, 1950, 15.1:1251-62.

830 Lederer, Ph. "Beiträge zur antiken Münzkunde. Blätter für Münzfreunde 16 (1924):165-71.

831 _____. "Seltene griechische Münzen der Sammlung Arthur von Gwinner." Berliner Münzblätter 35-37 (1914-1916):573-79.

832 Lehmann-Hartleben, Karl. Die antiken Hafenanlagen des Mittelmeeres. Beiträge zur Geschichte des Städtebaues im Altertum. Klio, Beiheft, 14. Leipzig: Dieterich'sche Verlagsbuchhandlung, 1923.

833 Lemerle, Paul. "À propos d'une basilique de Thasos et de Saint-Jean d'Ephèse." Byzantion 23 (1953):531-43.

834 Lenormant, François. "Les magistrats monétaires chez les Grecs." Mélanges de numismatique 3 (1882):1-51.

835 Le Rider, Georges. "Numismatique grecque." Annuaire de l'Ecole pratique des hautes études, Section des sciences historiques et philologiques (1972-1973):243-59.

836 Lesky, Albin. "Zu einem ephesischen Graffito." Wiener Studien n.f. 7 (1973):240-43.

837 Lessing, Erich, and Oberleitner, Wolfgang. Ephesos. Weltstadt der Antike. Heidelberg: Überreuter, 1978.

838 Lethaby, William R. "Another Note on the Sculpture of the Later Temple of Artemis at Ephesus." Journal of Hellenic Studies 36 (1916):25-35.

839 _____. "The Earlier Temple of Artemis at Ephesus." Journal of Hellenic Studies 37 (1917):1-16.

840 _____. "Further Notes on the Sculpture of the Later Temple of Artemis at Ephesus." Journal of Hellenic Studies 34 (1914):76-88.

841 _____. Greek Buildings represented by fragments in the British Museum. London: B. T. Batsford, 1908, pp. 1-36.

842 _____. "The hellenistic temple at Ephesus." The Builder (1920):147-50.

843 _____. "More Greek Studies VIII, The hellenistic Temple at Ephesus." The Builder (1929):566-68.

844 _____. "The Sculptures of the Later Temple of Artemis at Ephesus." Journal of Hellenic Studies 33 (1913):87-96.

845 _____. "The Sculptures of the Later Temple of Artemis at Ephesus." Journal of Hellenic Studies 34 (1914):76-88.

846 _____. "The Sculptures of the Later Temple of Artemis at Ephesus." Journal of Hellenic Studies 36 (1916):25-35.

847 _____. "The temple of Artemis at Ephesus." Journal of the Royal Institute of British Architects 22 (1915): 164.

848 Lévy, Isidore. "Etudes sur la vie municipale de l'Asie Mineure sous les Antonins; première série: l'ecclesia, la Boulé, la Gerousia." Revue des études grecques 8 (1895):203-50.

849 _____. "Etudes sur la vie municipale de l'Asie Mineure sous les Antonins; seconde série: les offices publics." Revue des études grecques 12 (1899):255-89.

850 Lewin, Thomas. The Life and Epistles of St. Paul. 5th ed. London: George Bell and Sons, 1890.

851 Lewis, Naphtali. Greek Historical Documents. The Roman Principate: 27 B.C.-285 A.D. Toronto: Hakkert, 1974, pp. 13, 17, 45, 87, 89, 105, 128-32.

852 Libertini, Guido. "Athena d'Efeso." Mitteilungen des Deutschen Archäologischen Instituts (Römische Abteilung) 40 (1925):125-35.

853 Lichtenecker, Elisabeth. "Die Kultbilder der Artemis von Ephesos." Dissertation, Tübingen University, 1952.

853a Lies, Lothar. Ephesos, Schnittpunkt von Antike und Christentum. Vienna: Gesellschaft der Freunde von Ephesos, 1985.

854 Lietzmann, Hans. "Die Umwelt des jungen Christentums." Die Antike 8 (1932):254-75.

855 Lightfoot, Joseph B. "Discoveries Illustrating the Acts of the Apostles." In Essays on the Word Entitled Supernatural Religion. London: Macmillan and Co., 1889, pp. 297-302.

856 _____. "On the Asiarchate." In The Apostolic
Fathers. 2nd ed. London: Macmillan and Co.,
1889, 3.2:404-15.

857 Lisičǎr. P. "Artemida Efeska i Dioskuri na votivnoj
steli u Bitoljskom muzeju." Živa antika 8 (1958):
305-09.

858 Löbbecke, A. "Griechische Münzen aus meiner Sammlung IV." Zeitschrift für Numismatik 17 (1890):1-26.

859 Löwy, Emanuel. "Again the temples of Ephesus."
Journal of Hellenic Studies 53 (1933):112.

860 _____. "Zur Chronologie der frühgriechischen
Kunst. Die Artemistempel von Ephesos." Anz. Wien
68 (1931):74.

861 _____. Zur Chronologie der frühgriechischen Kunst.
Die Artemistempel von Ephesos. Sitzungsberichte
der Akademie der Wissenschaften (philosophisch-
historische Klasse) 213.4. Vienna: Hölder-Pichler-
Tempsky, 1932.

862 L'Orange, Hans P. "L'origine ellenistico-romano del
ritratto bizantino." Corsi di cultura sull'arte ravennate e bizantina 17 (1970):253-56.

863 _____. Studien zur Geschichte des spätantiken
Porträts. Instituttet For Sammenlignende Kultur-
forskning, 22. Oslo: H. Aschehoug & Co., 1933.

864 Lucas, Hans. "Die Ganymedesstatue von Ephesos."
JÖAI 9 (1906):269-77.

865 Maccanico, Rosanna. "Ginnasi Romani ad Efeso."
Archeologia Classica 15 (1963):32-60.

866 MacDonald, George. Catalogue of Greek Coins in the
Hunterian collection. Vols. 2-3. Glasgow: J.
Maclehose and Sons, 1899-1905.

Magdalino, Paul. See no. 419.

867 Magie, David. Roman Rule in Asia Minor. 2 vols.
Princeton: Princeton University Press, 1950.

868 Maier, Franz G. Griechische Mauerbauinschriften.
Part 1. Texte und Kommentare. Vestigia.
Beiträge zur alten Geschichte, 1. Heidelberg:
Quelle & Meyer, 1959, pp. 236-42.

869 Maisonneuve, Henri. "S. Paul à Ephèse." Bible et
Terre Sainte 13 (1958):6-13.

870 Manganaro, Giacomo. "SGDI IV,4 n49 (DGE 707) e il
bimetallismo monetale di Creso." Epigraphica 36
(1974):57-77.

871 Mangold, Wilhelm M. "Ephesus." In Bibellexikon.
Realwörterbuch zum Handgebrauch für geistliche und
Gemeindeglieder. Edited by D. Schenkel. Leipzig:
Brockhaus, 1869, 2:127-32.

872 Mansel, Arif M. "Die neuesten Funde und Forschungen
in Kleinasien auf dem Gebiet der klassischen Archäologie und deren Probleme." In Atti del settimo
Congresso internazionale di Archeologia classica.
Rome: L'Erma, 1961, 1:304-305.

873 _____. "Villes mortes d'Asie Mineure occidentale."
Corsi di cultura sull'arte ravennate e bizantina 12
(1965):495-540.

874 Marcovich, Miroslav. "A New Graffito from Ephesos."
Greek, Roman and Byzantine Studies 14 (1973):61-63.

875 _____. "Three New Epigrams from Ephesus." ZPE
56 (1984):237-39.

Maresch, Gustav. See no. 731.

876 Masouris, Dem. S. "Ephesia grammata." Platon 18
(1966):304-16.

877 Massignon, Louis. Les sept dormants d'Ephèse (Ahl-al-
Kahf) en Islam et en Chrétienté. Paris: Librairie
orientaliste Paul Geuthner, 1955-63.

878 Masterplan for Protection and Use. Ephesus Historical
National Park, 1970.

879 Mattingly, Harold. Coins of the Roman Empire in the
British Museum. Reprinted with revisions. London:
British Museum, 1975- .

880 Mattingly, Harold, and Sutherland, Carol H. V. The
Roman Imperial Coinage. London: Spink, 1923-1981.

880a Mauterer, Richard. "Analysen ephesischer Elektronge-
genstände." Anz. Wien 119 (1982):65-8.

881 _____. "Archäologie und Archäometrie. Analytische
Chemie in der Archäometrie am Beispiel der Tetra-
drachmen aus Ephesos." In Lebendige Altertumswissenschaft. Festgabe zur Vollendung des 70. Lebensjahres von Hermann Vetters dargebracht von Freunden, Schülern und Kollegen. Vienna: Verlag Adolf
Holzhausens Nfg., 1985, pp. 417-19.

882 McCown, Chester C. "The Ephesia Grammata in Popular
Belief." Transactions and Proceedings of the American Philological Association 54 (1923):128-40.

883 M'Clintock, John, and Strong, James. "Ephesus."
Cyclopaedia of Biblical, Theological, and Ecclesiasti-
cal Literature. New York: Harper & Brothers, Pub-
lishers, 1878, 3:241-47.

McNicoll, Anthony W. See no. 1013.

884 Meinardus, Otto F. A. "The Alleged Advertisement
for the Ephesian Lupanar." Wiener Studien n.f. 7
(1973):244-48.

885 _____. "The Christian Remains of the Seven Churches
of the Apocalypse." Biblical Archaeologist 37 (1974):
71-75.

886 _____. St. John of Patmos and the Seven Churches
of the Apocalypse. Athens: Lycabettus Press, 1974.
pp. 33-59.

887 _____. St. Paul in Ephesus and the Cities of Galatia

and Cyprus. Athens: Lycabettus Press, 1973, pp. 51-129.

888 Meischner, Jutta. "Fragen zur römischen Porträtge-schichte, unter besonderer Berücksichtigung kleinasiatischer Beispiele." Bonner Jahrbücher 181 (1981):143-67.

889 Mellaart, James. "Deities and Shrines of Neolithic Anatolia: Excavations at Catal Hüyük, 1962." Archaeology 16.1 (1963):29-38.

890 Mellink, Machteld J. "Archaeology in Asia Minor." AJA 60 (1956):382.

891 _____. "Archaeology in Asia Minor." AJA 62 (1958):91-104.

892 _____. "Archaeology in Asia Minor." AJA 63 (1959):73-85.

893 _____. "Archaeology in Asia Minor." AJA 64 (1960):66-67.

894 _____. "Archaeology in Asia Minor." AJA 66 (1962):82-83.

895 _____. "Archaeology in Asia Minor." AJA 67 (1963):186-87.

896 _____. "Archaeology in Asia Minor." AJA 68 (1964):157-58.

897 _____. "Archaeology in Asia Minor." AJA 69 (1965):146-47.

898 _____. "Archaeology in Asia Minor." AJA 70 (1966):156-57.

899 _____. "Archaeology in Asia Minor." AJA 71 (1967):169.

900 _____. "Archaeology in Asia Minor." AJA 72 (1968):140-41.

901 _____. "Archaeology in Asia Minor." AJA 73 (1969):221.

902 _____. "Archaeology in Asia Minor." AJA 74 (1970):172.

903 _____. "Archaeology in Asia Minor." AJA 75 (1971):175-76.

904 _____. "Archaeology in Asia Minor." AJA 76 (1972):182-83.

905 _____. "Archaeology in Asia Minor." AJA 77 (1973):185-86.

906 _____. "Archaeology in Asia Minor." AJA 78 (1974):123-24.

907 _____. "Archaeology in Asia Minor." AJA 79 (1975):215.

908 _____. "Archaeology in Asia Minor." AJA 81 (1977):308.

909 _____. "Archaeology in Asia Minor." AJA 82 (1978):327-28.

910 _____. "Archaeology in Asia Minor." AJA 83 (1979):339.

911 _____. "Archaeology in Asia Minor." AJA 84 (1980):513.

912 _____. "Archaeology in Asia Minor." AJA 85 (1981):473.

913 _____. "Archaeology in Asia Minor." AJA 86 (1982):569.

914 _____. "Archaeology in Asia Minor." AJA 87 (1983):439-40.

915 _____. "Archaeology in Asia Minor." AJA 88 (1984):455.

916 _____. "A votive bird from Anatolia." Expedition
6.2 (1964):28-32.

917 Mellor, Ronald. Thea Rhome. The Worship of the
Goddess Roma in the Greek World. Hypomnemata:
Untersuchungen zur Antike und zu ihrer Nachleben,
42. Göttingen: Vandenhoeck & Ruprecht, 1975.

918 Menadier, Julius. Qua condicione Ephesii usi sint inde
ab Asia in formam provinciae redacta. Berlin:
Gustavus Schade, 1880.

919 Menestrier, Claude F. Symbolica Dianae Ephesiae
statua exposita. Rome: 1657.

920 Meriç, Recep. "Metrologische Funde aus Metropolis
und Ephesos." ZPE 41 (1981):211-15.

921 _____. "Metropolis, eine feldarchäologische Landauf-
nahme." Dissertation, University of Vienna, 1977.

922 _____. Metropolis in Ionien. Ergebnisse einer
Survey-Unternehmung in den Jahren 1972-1975.
Beiträge zur klassischen Philologie, 142. Königstein/
Ts: Verlag Anton Hain, 1982.

923 _____. "Metropolis'deki Satih Çalişmasi Hakkinda Ön
Rapor." Efes Harabeleri ve Müzesi Yilliği 1 (1972):
70-75.

924 _____. "Rekonstruktionsversuch der Kolossalstatue
des Domitian in Ephesos." In Pro Arte Antiqua.
Festschrift für Hedwig Kenner. 2: At Press.
Sonderschriften herausgegeben vom Österreichischen
Archäologischen Institut, 18, Vienna: Verlag A. F.
Koska.

925 _____. "Zur Lage des ephesischen Aussenhafens
Panormos." In Lebendige Altertumswissenschaft.
Festgabe zur Vollendung des 70. Lebensjahres von
Hermann Vetters dargebracht von Freunden, Schülern
und Kollegen. Vienna: Verlag Adolf Holzhausens
Nfg., 1985, pp. 30-32.

_____. See nos. 624, 769, 1378.

926 Meriç, Recep; Merkelbach, Reinhold; Nollé, Johannes;
and Şahin, Sencer, eds. Inschriften griechischer
Städte aus Kleinasien. vol. XVII,1: Die Inschriften
von Ephesos. 7,1: Nr. 3001-3500 (Repertorium).
Bonn: Habelt, 1981.

927 _____. Inschriften griechischer Städte aus Kleinasien.
XVII,2: Die Inschriften von Ephesos. 7,2: Nr.
3501-5110 (Repertorium). Bonn: Habelt, 1981.

928 Merkelbach, Reinhold. "Eigentor des grossen Rezensen-
ten." ZPE 37 (1980):76.

929 _____. "Ephesische Parerga 1. Der Proconsul A.
Vicirius Martialis." ZPE 24 (1977):150.

930 _____. "Ephesische Parerga 2. Der volle Name des
Flavius Cyrus, cos. 441." ZPE 24 (1977):164.

931 _____. "Ephesische Parerga 3. Eine weitere Frau
als theoros bei den ephesischen Olympien." ZPE 24
(1977):178.

932 _____. "Ephesische Parerga 4. Die Familie des
Aurelius Daphnus." ZPE 24 (1977):185-86.

933 _____. "Ephesische Parerga 5. aitesimos." ZPE 24
(1977):217-18.

934 _____. "Ephesische Parerga 6. Fragment eines
Epigramms auf Damocharis." ZPE 24 (1977):255.

935 _____. "Ephesische Parerga 7. Fragment einer
Ehreninschrift für den Pankratiasten und Boxer M.
Aurelius Demostratus Damas." ZPE 24 (1977):256.

936 _____. "Ephesische Parerga 8. Ein Chrysophoros."
ZPE 25 (1977):184.

937 _____. "Ephesische Parerga 9. Zum Erlass des
Proconsuls L. Antonius Albus über die Freihaltung
des Hafens." ZPE 25 (1977):208-09.

938 _____. "Ephesische Parerga 10. Die Weihinschrift
an der Osthalle der Agora." ZPE 25 (1977):280.

939 _____. "Ephesische Parerga 11. Ehrendekret für einen Getreidehändler aus Metropolis in Ionien." ZPE 26 (1977):152-53.

940 _____. "Ephesische Parerga 12. Eine tabula lusoria für den ludus latrunculorum." ZPE 28 (1978):48-50.

941 _____. "Ephesische Parerga 13. Der Prytanis und Hierokeryx Fabius Faustinianus." ZPE 28 (1978): 82-83.

942 _____. "Ephesische Parerga 14. Das Fest der dritten Neokorie und die Ehrenstatue der Stadt Karthagina." ZPE 28 (1978):96-98.

943 _____. "Ephesische Parerga 15. Fine Ehreninschrift für Cn. Pompeius Hermippus Aelianus." ZPE 28 (1978):108.

944 _____. "Ephesische Parerga 16. Eine Inschrift vom Agon der Ärzte." ZPE 29 (1978):148.

945 _____. "Ephesische Parerga 17. Epigramm auf einen Gladiator." ZPE 29 (1978):210.

946 _____. "Ephesische Parerga 18. Der Bäckerstreik." ZPE 30 (1978):164-65.

947 _____. "Ephesische Parerga 19. Eine weitere Inschrift des L. Antonius." ZPE 31 (1978):36-37.

948 _____. "Ephesische Parerga 20. Grabstein des Exakestas und der Pothusa." ZPE 31 (1978):70.

949 _____. "Ephesische Parerga 21. Ein Zeugnis für Ti. Claudius Balbillus aus Smyrna." ZPE 31 (1978): 186-87.

950 _____. "Ephesische Parerga 22. Die Bauinschrift des byzantinischen Aquaeductes." ZPE 32 (1978):44.

951 _____. "Ephesische Parerga 23. Pedion Maiandrion." ZPE 32 (1978):212.

952 _____. "Ephesische Parerga 24. Menaitetos." ZPE 32 (1978):232.

953 _____. "Ephesische Parerga 25. Commodus als Bruder des Septimius Severus." ZPE 33 (1979): 189-90.

954 _____. "Ephesische Parerga 26. Warum Domitians Siegername 'Germanicus' eradiert worden ist." ZPE 34 (1979): 62-64.

955 _____. "Die ephesische Prytanin Tullia." ZPE 9 (1972): 76.

956 _____. "Die ephesischen Dionysosmysten vor der Stadt." ZPE 36 (1979): 151-56.

957 _____. "Die ephesischen Monate in der Kaiserzeit." ZPE 36 (1979): 157-62.

958 _____. "Epigramm auf Eulalios." ZPE 10 (1973): 70.

959 _____. "Gefesselte Götter." Antaios 12 (1971): 549-65.

960 _____. "Der Kult der Hestia im Prytaneion der griechischen Städte." ZPE 37 (1980): 77-92.

961 _____. "OLYMPEIEIA." ZPE 12 (1973): 210.

962 _____. "Der Rangstreit der Städte Asiens und die Rede des Aelius Aristides über die Eintracht." ZPE 32 (1978): 287-96.

963 _____. "Über ein ephesisches Dekret für einen Athleten aus Aphrodisias und über den Athletentitel PARADOXOS." ZPE 14 (1974): 91-96.

_____. See nos. 174, 302, 362, 770, 771, 772, 773, 774, 775, 776, 777.

964 Merkelbach, Reinhold, and Nollé, Johannes, eds. Inschriften griechischer Städte aus Kleinasien. XVI: Die Inschriften von Ephesos. 6: Nr. 2001-2958 (Repertorium). Mit Hilfe von Englemann, H. Bonn: Habelt, 1980.

965 _____. Inschriften griechischer Städte aus Klein-

asien: Addenda et Corrigenda zu den Inschriften
von Ephesos I-VII, 1 (IK 11, 1-17, 1). Bonn:
Habelt, 1981.

966 Merkelbach, Reinhold, and Şahin, Sencer. "Die
Siklianoi bei Ephesos." ZPE 32 (1978):286.

967 Metcalf, William E. "Hadrian, Iovis Olympius."
Mnemosyne 27 (1974):59-66.

968 Metzger, Bruce M. "A Magical Amulet for Curing Fever."
In Historical and Literary Studies. Pagan, Jewish,
and Christian. New Testament Tools and Studies, 8.
Edited by Bruce M. Metzger. Grand Rapids: Wm. B.
Eerdmans, 1968, pp. 104-110.

969 Metzger, Henri. St. Paul's Journeys in the Greek
Orient. London: SCM Press, Ltd., 1955.

970 Metzler, Dieter. "Ein Meisterwerk spätantiker Porträt-
kunst." Archäologischer Anzeiger 84 (1969):195-203.

971 Meurer, M. "Die mammae der Artemis Ephesia."
Mitteilungen des Deutschen Archäologischen Instituts
(Römische Abteilung) 29 (1914):200-19.

972 Michaelis, Wilhelm. "Das Gefängnis des Paulus in
Ephesus." Byzantinisch-neugriechische Jahrbücher
6 (1927-1928):1-18.

973 Mielsch, Harald. "Proteus und Menelaos. Ein anton-
inisches Gemälde in Ephesos." Archäologischer
Anzeiger (1980):550-53.

974 Millar, Fergus. The Emperor in the Roman World.
Ithaca: Cornell University Press, 1977.

975 Miller, Daniel L. The Seven Churches of Asia:
Ephesus, Smyrna, Pergamos, Thyatira, Sardis,
Philadelphia, Laodicea. Elgin: Brethren Publish-
ing House, 1907, pp. 27-53.

976 Miller, Stephen G. "Drinking Uncut Wine ... to Death.
Unpublished Greek Epigram for a Youth from
Ephesus." Ancient World 2 (1979):29-30.

977 _____. The Prytaneion. Its Function and Architectural Form. Los Angeles: University of California
Press, 1978, pp. 98-109.

978 Milne, Joseph G. "J. T. Wood's Coins from Ephesus."
Numismatic Chronicle 5th. ser. 5 (1925):385-91.

979 _____. "Notes on the Oxford Collections, 3. Ionia."
Numismatic Chronicle 5th ser. 17 (1937):153-81.

980 Miltner, Franz. "Die Ausgrabungen von Ephesos."
Die Denkmalpflege 6 (1932):100-106.

981 _____. "Bericht über die Ausgrabungen in Ephesos
1955." Türk Arkeoloji Dergisi 7.1 (1957):13-19.

982 _____. (+) "Bericht über die Ausgrabungen in
Ephesos 1956." Türk Arkeoloji Dergisi 7.1 (1957):
20-25.

983 _____. "Bericht über die österreichischen Ausgrabungen in Ephesos im Jahre 1957." Anz. Wien 95 (1958):
79-89.

984 _____. (+) "Bericht über die österreichischen Ausgrabungen in Ephesos im Jahre 1957." Türk Arkeoloji Dergisi 8.1 (1958):19-25.

985 _____. "Denkmalpflege in Ephesos." Österreichische
Zeitschrift für Kunst und Denkmalpflege 13 (1959):
1-10.

986 _____. "Dionysos' Kindheit als Lampenbild." JÖAI
27 (1932):174.

987 _____. "Ephesos, die Stadt der Artemis und des
Johannes, Österreichs Ausgrabungsstätte in Anatolien." Atlantis 30 (1958):307-14.

988 _____. Ephesos. Stadt der Artemis und des Johannes.
Vienna: F. Deuticke, 1958.

989 _____. "Ephesus. Summary of Archaeological Research in Turkey in 1957." Anatolian Studies 8
(1958):27-28.

990 _____. "Ephesus. Summary of Archaeological Research in Turkey in 1958." Anatolian Studies 9 (1959):22-24.

991 _____. "Epigraphe ex Ephesou (Symbole eis tas anaskaphas tou naou tou Theologou en Epheso)." Deltion 9 (1924-1925):118-20.

992 _____. "Ergebnisse der österreichischen Ausgrabungen in Ephesos im Jahre 1955." Anz. Wien 93 (1956): 43-52.

993 _____. "Ergebnisse der österreichischen Ausgrabungen in Ephesos im Jahre 1956." Anz. Wien 94 (1957):13-25.

994 _____. Forschungen in Ephesos. vol. 4.2 Das Cömeterium der Sieben Schläfer. Baden at Vienna: Rudolf M. Rohrer, 1937.

995 _____. "Grabungsergebnisse in Ephesos im Frühjahr 1954." Anz. Wien 91 (1954):249-51.

996 _____. "I grandiosi scavi de Efeso cristiana." Illustrazione Vaticana 4 (1933):883-85.

997 _____. "Die Marienkirche von Ephesos." Kirchenkunst 3 (1931):23-27.

998 _____. "Die neuen Artemisstatuen aus Ephesos." Anatolia 3 (1958):21-34.

999 _____. "Die neuen Ausgrabungen in Ephesos." Mitteilungen, Deutsch-türkische Gesellschaft 15 (1957):1-5.

1000 _____. "Die österreichischen Ausgrabungen des Jahres 1958 in Ephesos." Türk Arkeoloji Dergisi 9.1 (1959):25-32.

1001 _____. "Die österreichischen Ausgrabungen in Ephesos." Vierteljahrsblätter der Trierer Gesellschaft für nützliche Forschungen 1 (1955):9-10.

1002 _____. "Die österreichischen Ausgrabungen in

Ephesos im Jahre 1958." Anz. Wien 96 (1959): 31-43.

1003 _____. "Eine Reliefplatte vom Tempel Hadrians in Ephesos." In Festschrift zu Ehren Richard Heuberger. Schlern-Schriften, 206. Innsbruck: Wagner, 1960, pp. 93-98.

1004 _____. "Reliefs mit Ausrüstungsstücken für Gladiatorenkämpfe und Naumachien." In Forschungen in Ephesos, vol. 4.3 Die Johannes-kirche. Vienna: Österreichisches Archäologisches Institut, 1951, pp. 268-74.

1005 _____. "Two new statues of Diana of the Ephesians, and other discoveries in the ancient city of Ephesus." Illustrated London News 232 (1958):221-23.

1006 _____. "XX. Vorläufiger Bericht über die Aus-grabungen in Ephesos." JÖAI 42 (1955):Beibl. 23-60.

1007 _____. "XXI. Vorläufiger Bericht über die Aus-grabungen in Ephesos." JÖAI 43 (1956-1958):Beibl. 1-64.

1008 _____. (+) "XXII. Vorläufiger Bericht über die Ausgrabungen in Ephesos." JÖAI 44 (1959):Beibl. 243-314.

1009 _____. (+) "XXIII. Vorläufiger Bericht über die Ausgrabungen in Ephesos." JÖAI 44 (1959):Beibl. 315-80.

1010 _____. (+) "XXIV. Vorläufiger Bericht über die Ausgrabungen in Ephesos." JÖAI 45 (1960):Beibl. 1-76.

1011 Mionnet, Theodore E. Description de médailles antiques, grecques et romaines. Paris: Testu, 1806-1822.

1012 _____. Description de médailles antiques, grecques et romaines. Supplément. Paris: Testu, 1819.

1013 Mitchell, S., and McNicoll, Anthony W. "Archaeology

in Western and Southern Asia Minor." The Journal
of Hellenic Studies. Archaeological Reports for
1978-79 25 (1979):71-73.

1014 Mitsopoulos-Leon, Veronika. "Ephesos." In The
Princeton Encyclopedia of Classical Sites. Edited
by R. Stillwell. Princeton: Princeton University
Press, 1976, pp. 306-10.

1015 _____. "Ein Grabfund des vierten vorchristlichen
Jahrhunderts aus Ephesos." JÖAI 50 (1972-1975):
252-65.

1016 _____. "Hellenistische Keramik mit Schlickerdekor
aus Ephesos und ihr Verhältnis zur attischen
'Westabhang-Keramik.'" In Classica et Provincialia.
Festschrift Erna Diez. Edited by G. Schwarz and
E. Pochmarski. Graz: Akademische Druck und
Verlagsanstalt, 1978, pp. 113-23.

1017 _____. "Keramik aus Basilika und Prytaneion--Ein
Überblick." JÖAI 50 (1972-1975):Grabungen in
Ephesos von 1960-1969 bzw. 1970, 495-524.

1018 _____. "Ein Metallvorbild für hellenistische
Tonschüsseln? Zu einer Henkelform aus Ephesos."
Archaiologika analekta ex Athenon 10 (1977):296-
302.

1019 _____. "Töpferateliers in Ephesos." In Pro Arte
Antiqua. Festschrift für Hedwig Kenner. 2: At
Press. Sonderschriften herausgegeben vom
Österreichischen Archäologischen Institut, 18.
Vienna: Verlag A. F. Koska.

1020 _____. "Zu den Einzelfunden." In Forschungen in
Ephesos, vol. 6 Das Mausoleum von Belevi. Vienna:
Österreichisches Archäologisches Institut, 1979,
pp. 161-66.

Möbius, Hans. See no. 1091.

1021 Mommsem, Theodor. "Volksbeschluss der Ephesier zu
Ehren des Kaisers Antoninus Pius." JÖAI 3 (1900):
1-8.

1022 Morawiecki, Lesław. "Le monoptère sur les monnaies
     alexandrines de bronze du temps d'Auguste." Eos
     64 (1976):59-82.

1023 Mørkholm, O. "Some Reflections on the Early Cisto-
     phoric Coinage." The American Numismatic Society
     Museum Notes 24 (1979):47-61.

1024 Moustier, A. de. Voyage de Constantinople à Ephèse
     par l'intermédiaire de l'Asie Mineure, Bithynie,
     Phrygie, Lydie, Ionie. Tour du Monde, 9. Paris:
     1864.

1025 Münsterberg, Rudolf. "Aus van Lenneps Nachlass."
     Numismatische Zeitschrift 48 (1915):108-116.

1026 _____. Die Beamtennamen auf den griechischen
     Münzen. Subsidia Epigraphica, 3. Hildesheim:
     George Olms Verlag, 1973, pp. 84-9, Nachtrag.
     p. 27.

1027 Murray, Alexander Stuart. "Remains of Archaic Tem-
     ple of Artemis at Ephesus." Journal of Hellenic
     Studies 10 (1889):1-10.

1028 _____. "The Sculptured Columns of the Temple of
     Diana at Ephesus." Journal of the Royal Institute
     of British Architects 3rd ser. 3 (1895-1896):41-57.

1029 Muss, Ulrike. "Studien zur Bauplastik des archaischen
     Artemisions von Ephesos." Dissertation, University
     of Bonn, 1983.

1030 Muth, Robert. "Essen." Anzeiger für die Altertums-
     wissenschaft 5 (1952):61-64; 123-128.

1031 Natterer, K. "Über Bronzen aus Ephesos." Akademie
     der Wissenschaften zu Wien. Sitzungsberichte der
     Philosophisch-historische Klasse 109.11 (1900):1-7.

1032 Naumann, Friederike. Die Ikonographie der Kybele in
     der phrygischen und der griechischen Kunst.
     Istanbuler Mitteilungen, Beiheft 28. Tübingen:
     Verlag Ernst Wasmuth, 1983.

Navarre, Octave. See no. 1136.

1033 Neumann, Günter. "Epigraphische Mitteilungen: Kleinasien." Kadmos 7 (1968):185-86.

1034 Neuss, W. "Forschungen in Ephesus." Das Münster 7 (1954):255-57.

1035 Newton, Charles. "On an electrum stater, possibly of Ephesus." Numismatic Chronicle 10 (1870):237-39.

Niemann, George. See nos. 519, 1501.

1036 Niemann, George, and Heberdey, Rudolf. "Der Rundbau auf dem Panajirdagh." In Forschungen in Ephesos. Vienna: Alfred Hölder, 1906, 1:143-80.

1037 Niemann, George, and Karabacek, Josef von. "Die seldschukischen Bauwerke in Ajasoluk." In Forschungen in Ephesos. Vienna: Alfred Hölder, 1906, 1:111-31.

1038 Niessen, Johannes. Ephesus. Die letzte Wohnstätte der hl. Jungfrau Maria. Münster: Aschendorff, 1931, pp. 51-62.

1039 Noack, Ferdinand. "Amazonenstudien." Jahrbuch des Deutschen Archäologischen Instituts 30 (1915):131-79.

Noe, Sydney P. See no. 741.

1040 Noll, Rudolf. "Frühbyzantinische Bronzestempel mit Inschriften aus Ephesos." In Lebendige Altertumswissenschaft. Festgabe zur Vollendung des 70. Lebensjahres von Hermann Vetters dargebracht von Freunden, Schülern und Kollegen. Vienna: Verlag Adolf Holzhausens Nfg., 1985, pp. 318-21.

1041 _____. Griechische und lateinische Inschriften der Wiener Antikensammlung. Vienna: Verlag Notring der wissenschaftlichen Verbände Österreichs, 1962, nos. 40-64.

1042 _____. Vom Altertum zum Mittelalter, Katalog der Antikensammlung I. 2nd ed. Führer durch das

Kunsthistorische Museum, 8. Vienna: Anton Schroll & Co., 1974.

1043 Nollé, Johannes. "Grabepigramme und Reliefdarstellungen aus Kleinasien." ZPE 60 (1985):133-35.

1044 _____. "Ofellius Laetus, platonischer Philosoph." ZPE 41 (1981):197-206.

_____. See nos. 210, 926, 927, 964, 965.

1045 Oakley, Kenneth P. "The Diopet of Ephesus." Folklore 82 (1971):207-11.

1046 Oberleitner, Wolfgang. "Beiträge zur Geschichte der spätantiken Porträtplastik aus Ephesos." JÖAI 47 (1964-1965):5-35.

1047 _____. "Bildnisse der Spätantike, erläutert an sechs Porträtkopfen im Wiener Kunsthistorischen Museum." Antike Welt 2.2 (1971):31-38.

1048 _____. "Drei unbekannte Köpfe des Partherdenkmals." In Pro Arte Antiqua. Festschrift für Hedwig Kenner. 2: At Press. Sonderschriften herausgegeben vom Österreichischen Archäologischen Institut, 18. Vienna: Verlag A. F. Koska.

1049 _____. "Fragment eines spätantiken Porträtkopfes aus Ephesos." JÖAI 44 (1959):83-100.

1050 _____. "Ein hellenistischer Galaterschlachtfries aus Ephesos." Jahrbuch der kunsthistorischen Sammlungen in Wien 77 (1981):57-104.

1051 _____. "Das neue Ephesos-Museum in Wien." Alte und Moderne Kunst 27, Heft 182 (1982):28-33.

1052 _____. "Römische und frühbyzantinische Porträts aus Ephesos." In Römische und frühbyzantinische Porträtplastik aus der Türkei. Neue Funde. Edited by J. Inan and E. Alföldi-Rosenbaum. Mainz: Zabern, 1979, pp. 104f; 109f; 184ff.

1053 _____. "Zur Echtheit eines Berliner Strategenkopfes." JÖAI 44 (1959):79-82.

1054 _____. "Zwei spätantike Kaiserköpfe aus Ephesos." Jahrbuch der kunsthistorischen Sammlungen in Wien 69 (1973):127-65.

_____. See no. 837.

1055 Oberleitner, Wolfgang; Gschwantler, Kurt; Bernhard-Walcher, Alfred; and Bammer, Anton. Funde aus Ephesos und Samothrake. Katalog der Antikensammlung, 2. Vienna: Kunsthistorisches Museum, 1978.

1056 Ocheşeanu, R. "Doi denari romani republicani descoperiţi în Dobrogea." Pontica 5 (1972):497-502.

1057 Önen, Ülgür. Ephesus, Ruins and Museum. The City's History through Art. Izmir: Akademia, 1983.

1058 _____. Ephesus, the Way it Was. The City Viewed in Reconstructions. Izmir: Akademia Tanitma Merkezi, 1985.

1059 "Österreichische Ausgrabungen in Ephesos." Die Bauzeitung (1928):441-44.

1060 Oettli, D. "Ein Besuch in Ephesus." Theologische Zeitschrift aus der Schweiz 10 (1893):149-56.

1061 Özeren, Öcal. "Selçuk Ilçe'sindeki Türk Hamamlari." Efes Müzesi Yilliği 2 (1973-1978):69-79.

1062 Özgan, Ramazan. Untersuchungen zur archaischen Plastik Ioniens. Bonn: Rheinische Friedrich-Wilhelms-Universität, 1983.

1063 Oikonomos, Georgios P. "Naopoioi kai Essenes." Deltion 7 (1921-1922):258-346.

1064 Oliver, James H. "On the Ephesian debtor law of 85 B.C." American Journal of Philology 60 (1939): 468-70.

1065 _____. The Sacred Gerusia. Hesperia Supplement,

6. Athens: American School of Classical Studies, 1941, pp. 53-106.

1066 Oliver, James H., and Swift, Louis J. "Constantius II on Falvius Philippus." American Journal of Philology 83 (1962):247-64.

1067 Oster, Richard E. "Christianity and Emperor Veneration in Ephesus: Iconography of a Conflict." Restoration Quarterly 25 (1982):143-49.

1068 _____. "The Ephesian Artemis as an Opponent of Early Christianity." Jahrbuch für Antike und Christentum 19 (1976):27-44.

1069 _____. "Ephesus as a Religious Center Under the Principate I. Paganism Before Constantine." In Aufstieg und Niedergang der römischen Welt. II 18.1: At press.

1070 _____. "A Historical Commentary on the Missionary Success Stories in Acts 19:11-40." Dissertation, Princeton Theological Seminary, 1974.

1071 _____. "Note on Acts 19:23-41 and an Ephesian Inscription." Harvard Theological Review 77 (1984):233-37.

1072 _____. "Numismatic Windows into the Social World of Early Christianity: A Methodological Inquiry." Journal of Biblical Literature 101-102 (1982):214-18.

1073 Pace, B. "Ephese." Anadolu 2 (1955):75-77.

1074- Pajakowski, W. "Odkrycia archeologiczne w Efezie."
75   Z Otchlani Wieków 24 (1958):279-81.

1076 Palma, Beatrice. "Efeso." In Enciclopedia dell'Arte Antica e Orientale. Supplement. Rome: Istituto Poligrafico Dello Stato, 1973, 1:289-92.

1077 Paper. "Die Spiele von Hierapolis." Zeitschrift für Numismatik 26 (1908):161-82.

1078 Paranika, M. "Peri Ephesou." Ho en Konstantinoupolei
 Hellenikos Philologikos Syllogos 14 (1884):49-60.

1079 Paribeni, Enrico. "Artemis the Multiple Goddess and
 the Didymaion." In VIII. Türk Tarih Kongresi.
 Türk Tarih Kurumu Yayinlari, 9.8. Ankara: Türk
 Tarih Kurumu Basimevi, 1979, 1:281-86.

1080 _____. "Di Diana Nemorensis e di Artemide Efesia."
 Dialoghi di Archeologia n.s. 3.1 (1981):41-48.

1081 Parlasca, Klaus. "Zur Artemis Ephesia als Dea Natura
 in der klassizistischen Kunst." In Studien zur
 Religion und Kultur Kleinasiens. Festschrift für
 Friedrich Karl Dörner zum 65. Geburtstag am 28.
 Februar 1976. Edited by S. Şahin, E. Schwertheim,
 and J. Wagner. EPRO, 66.2. Leiden: E. J. Brill,
 1978, 2:679-89.

1082 Parvis, Merrill M. "Archaeology and St. Paul's Journeys in Greek Lands. Part IV--Ephesus." Biblical
 Archaeologist 8 (1945):62-73.

1083 Peek, Werner. "Zu dem neuen Grabepigramm aus
 Ephesos ZPE 21, 191f." ZPE 28 (1978):178-79.

1084 _____. "Zu einem Gladiatoren-Epigramm aus
 Ephesos." ZPE 32 (1978):6.

1085 Pekáry, Thomas. "Statuen in kleinasiatischen Inschriften." In Studien zur Religion und Kultur Kleinasiens. Festschrift für Friedrich Karl Dörner zum
 65. Geburtstag am 28 Februar 1976. Edited by S.
 Şahin, E. Schwertheim, and J. Wagner. EPRO,
 66.2. Leiden: E. J. Brill, 1978, 2:727-44.

1086 Petzl, Georg. "Epheso-Smyrnaicum." ZPE 31 (1978):
 227-28.

1087 _____. "Reste eines ephesischen Exemplars des
 Senatusconsultum de agro Pergameno (Sherk, Rom.
 Doc. 12)." Epigraphica Anatolica 6 (1985):70-71.

1088 Pfeiffer, Charles F., and Vos, Howard F. The Wycliffe

Historical Geography of Bible Lands. Chicago:
Moody Press, 1967, pp. 357-65.

1089 Pflaum, Hans G. "Un nouveau censeur de la Gaule
lyonnaise à la lumière d'une inscription du IIIe s.
provenant de la région d'Ephèse." Bulletin de la
Société Nationale des Antiquaires de France (1966):
40-41.

1090 _____. "Vibius Seneca, dux vexillationum classis
praetoriae Misenatium et Ravennensium." Studi
Romagnoli 18 (1967):255-57.

1091 Pfuhl, Ernst (+), and Möbius, Hans. Die ostgriech-
ischen Grabreliefs. 4 vols. Mainz: Verlag Philipp
von Zabern, 1977-79.

1092 Phaedros, G. Guide book of the ruins of Ephesus.
Smyrna: 1910.

1093 Philippson, Alfred. "Antike Stadtlagen an der Westküste Kleinasiens." Bonner Jahrbücher 123 (1916):
109-131.

1094 Picard, Charles. "Au plafond de la Chambre de la
Signature (Vatican): l'Allégorie de la Philosophie
sur son trône évoquant l''Ephesia.'" Revue
archéologique (1963):64-68.

1095 _____. "De l'incendie de l'Artémision d'Ephèse au
sac des Palais de Persépolis." Comptes rendus de
l'Académie des Inscriptions et Belles-Lettres (1956):
81-99.

1096 _____. "D'Ephèse à la Gaule, et de Stobi (Macédoine)
à Claros." Revue des études grecques 70 (1957):
108-117.

1097 _____. Ephèse et Claros. Recherches sur les
Sanctuaires et les Cultes de L'Ionie du Nord.
Paris: E. De Boccard, 1922.

1098 _____. "L'Ephesia, les Amazones et les Abeilles."
In Mélanges d'Etudes anciennes offerts à Georges
Radet. Paris: Klincksieck, 1940, pp. 270-84
[=Revue des études anciennes, 42].

1099 _____ . "Die Ephesia von Anatolien." In Eranos-
Jahrbuch. Zurich: Rhein Verlag, 1938, 6:59-90.

1100 _____ . "Les inscriptions du théâtre d'Ephèse et le
culte d'Artémis Ephesia." Revue de philologie 37
(1913):76-94.

1101 _____ . "Le mausolée de Bélèvi (près d'Ephèse)."
Revue archéologique 6th ser. 2 (1933):332-33.

1102 _____ . "Notes d'archéologie Grecque, B. Bomospeira
d'Ionie, et 'columnae caelatae.'" Revue des études
anciennes 29 (1927):255-73.

1103 _____ . "Percées tympanales, ou niches de fronton?"
Revue archéologique 6th ser. 34 (1949):19-39.

1104 _____ . "Le plastron rituel de la statue de culte de
l'Artémis Ephésia était-il garni d'oeufs d'autruche?"
Revue archéologique (1962):103-106.

1105 _____ . "Sur les reconstructions de l'Artémision
d'Ephèse." Laographia 7 (1923):69ff.

1106 _____ . "Sur une figurine de bronze argenté
trouvée à Tell el Farah, près de Naplouse (Palestine)." Revue archéologique (1958):91-3.

1107 _____ . "Les 'symplegmata' du gymnase hellénistico-
romain d'Ephèse et la décoration statuaire des
édifices de sport à l'époque romaine impériale."
Comptes rendus de l'Académie des Inscriptions et
Belles-Lettres (1955):20-32.

1108 Picard, Gilbert-Charles. "Le monument de César
Cosmocratôr au Capitole." Revue archéologique
n.s. 1 (1973):261-72.

1109 Pick, Behrendt. "Die Neokorien von Ephesos." In
Corolla Numismatica. Numismatic Essays in honour
of Barclay V. Head. Oxford: H. Frowde, 1906,
pp. 234-44.

1110 _____ . "Die Tempeltragenden Gottheiten und die
Darstellung der Neokorie auf den Münzen." JÖAI
7 (1904):1-41.

1111 Picón, Carlos A. "The Sculptures of the Archaic
Temple of Artemis at Ephesos." AJA 87 (1983):251.

1112 Pleket, H. William. "An Aspect of the Imperial Cult:
Imperial Mysteries." Harvard Theological Review
58 (1965):331-47.

1113 _____. "Frustula epigraphica Asiae Minoris. II.
Hierourgoi Bou(leutai): A note on the status of
cult servants in the Ephesian Prytaneion."
Epigraphica Anatolica 1 (1983):104-06.

1114 Plommer, Hugh. "St. John's Church, Ephesus."
Anatolian Studies 12 (1962):119-29.

1115 Pochmarski, Erwin. "Ein Kinderkopf (Eros?) aus
Ephesos." In Pro Arte Antiqua. Festschrift für
Hedwig Kenner. 2: At Press. Sonderschriften
herausgegeben vom Österrichischen Archäologischen
Institut, 18 Vienna: Verlag A. F. Koska.

1116 Poerner, Johannes. "De Curetibus et Corybantibus."
Dissertation, University of Halle, 1913.

1117 Poleni, G. "Osoervazioni sopra un passos di Plinio
risguardante la costruzione del tempio di Diana
Efesia. Lib. 36. Cap. 14." Memorie per le Belle
Arti 2 (1786):187-94.

1118 _____. "Sopra al tempio di Diana d'Efeso." Saggi
di Cortona I, 2 (1742):1-64.

1119 Praschniker, Camillo. (+) "Die Datierung." In
Forschungen in Ephesos. vol. 6 Das Mausoleum von
Belevi. Vienna: Österreichisches Archäologisches
Institut, 1979, pp. 109-20.

1120 _____. "Die Datierung des Mausoleums von Belevi."
Anz. Wien 85 (1948):271-93.

1121 _____. (+) "Die Einzelfunde." In Forschungen in
Ephesos. vol. 6 Das Mausoleum von Belevi.
Vienna: Österreichisches Archäologisches Institut,
1979, pp. 105-108.

1122 _____. (+) "Der figürliche Schmuck." In
Forschungen in Ephesos. vol. 6 Das Mausoleum von
Belevi. Vienna: Österreichisches Archäologisches
Institut, 1979, pp. 73-104.

1123 _____. "Der Hermes des Alkamenes in Ephesos."
JÖAI 29 (1935):23-31.

1124 _____. "Die Skulpturen des Mausoleum von Belevi."
In Bericht über den VI. Internationalen Kongress
für Archäologie (Berlin 21.-26. August 1939).
Edited by M. Wegner. Berlin: Walter de Gruyter
& Co., 1940, pp. 405-06.

1125 Praschniker, Camillo, and Theuer, Max. eds.
Forschungen in Ephesos. vol. 6 Das Mausoleum
von Belevi. Vienna: Österreichisches Archäologisches Institut, 1979.

1126 Price, Martin J. "Greek Imperial Coins. Some Recent
Acqusitions by the British Museum." Numismatic
Chronicle 7th ser. 11 (1971):121-34.

1127 Price, Martin J., and Trell, Bluma L. Coins and
Their Cities. Architecture on the Ancient Coins
of Greece, Rome, and Palestine. Detroit: Wayne
State University Press, 1977, pp. 127-32.

1128 Price, Simon R. F. Rituals and Power. The Roman
Imperial Cult in Asia Minor. New York: Cambridge
University Press, 1984.

1129 Prins de Jong, Elisabeth. F. "De Stad Ephesus."
Hermeneus 7 (1934-35):7-12.

1130 Prskawetz, A. K. "Baugeschichtsforschung nicht nur
im Interesse des Historikers." Antike Welt 7.3
(1976):16-18.

1131 Pryce, Frederick N. Catalogue of Sculpture in the
Department of Greek and Roman Antiquities of the
British Museum. Oxford: Oxford University
Press, 1928, 1.1:32-98.

1132 Psalty, Fr. "Les ruines de la maison de la Vierge

Marie à Panaya-Capouli." In Actes du Xe Congrès
International d'Etudes Byzantines Istanbul 15-21 IX
1955. Istanbul, ca. 1956, pp. 152-57.

1133 Puchstein, O. "Antike Dachziegel aus Ephesus."
Archäologischer Anzeiger 5 (1890):161-63.

1134 Radet, Georges. Ephesiaca. I. La topographie
d'Ephèse. II. La colonisation d'Ephèse par les
Ioniens. Bordeaux: Feret et Fils, 1908.

1135 _____. "Recherches sur la géographie ancienne de
l'Asie Mineure. IV. La colonisation d'Ephèse par
les Ioniens." Revue des études anciennes 8
(1906):1-22.

1135a _____. "La topographie d'Ephèse." Journal des
savants n.f. 1 (1906):251-64.

1136 Radet, Georges; Navarre, Octave; and Fournier, Paul.
"Le théâtre d'Ephèse." Revue des études anciennes
15 (1913):313-30.

Radt, Wolfgang. See no. 781.

1137 Ramsay, William M. "Anatolica Quaedam (V. Medical
Prescriptions at Holy Places)." Journal of Hellenic
Studies 50 (1930):264-66.

1138 _____. "Artemis at Ephesus." Classical Review 7
(1893):78-79.

1139 _____. The Church in the Roman Empire before
A.D. 70. 5th ed. Grand Rapids: Baker Book
House, 1954, pp. 112-45.

1140 _____. "Ephesus." In A Dictionary of the Bible.
Edited by J. Hastings. Edinburgh: T & T Clark,
1898, 1:720-25.

1141 _____. "Ephesus." Biblical World 17 (1901):167-77.

1142 _____. "Ephesus: Damascus. Rock Milestone near
Kabatia." Athenaeum, May 21, 1898.

1143 _____. "The Lawful Assembly (Acts 19.39)." In
Pauline and Other Studies in Early Christian History.
London: Hodder and Stoughton, 1906, pp. 203-15.

1144 _____. "The Letters to the Seven Churches of
Asia." Expositor 6th ser. 9 (1904): pt. 8 "The
Letter to the Church in Ephesus":170-73; pt. 9
"The Letter to the Church in Ephesus (continued).":
241-48; pt. 10 "Peroration of the Ephesian Letter.":
248-50; and pt. 11 "Character of the Letter to the
Church in Ephesus.":250-56.

1145 _____. The Letters to the Seven Churches of Asia
and Their Place in the Plan of Apocalypse. London:
Hodder and Stoughton, 1904, pp. 210-50.

1145a _____. "Sketches in the Religious Antiquities of
Asia Minor." The Annual of the British School at
Athens 18 (1911-1912): pt. 13 "The Ephesian Arte-
mis at Saghir near Antioch.":67-70.

1146 _____. "St. Paul at Ephesus." The Expositor 4th
ser. 2 (1890):1-22.

1147 _____. St. Paul the Traveller and the Roman
Citizen. 3rd ed. Grand Rapids: Baker Book
House, 1951, pp. 262-82.

1148 _____. "The Worship of the Virgin Mary at Ephesus."
Expositor 6th ser. 11 (1905): pt. 1 "General Statement of the Situation":401-5; pt. 2 "The Survival
of Pagan Cults":405-15; and pt. 3 "Early Worship
of the Mother of God in Ephesus" 6th. ser. 12
(1905):81-98.

1149 _____. "The Worship of the Virgin Mary at Ephesus."
In Pauline and Other Studies in Early Christian History. London: Hodder and Stoughton, 1906, pp.
125-59.

1150 Regling, Kurt. "Syrien, nicht Ephesos." Zeitschrift
für Numismatik 32 (1915):146-52.

1151 _____. "Zur griechischen Münzkunde II."
Zeitschrift für Numismatik 23 (1902):190-202.

1152 Reinach, Adolphe. "La fondation de P. Vibius Salutaris à Ephèse." Revue épigraphique 1 (1913):227-
38.

1153 Reisch, Emil. "Die Grabungen des österreichischen
archäologischen Institutes während der Jahre 1912
und 1913." JÖAI 16 (1913):Beibl. 89-92.

1154 _____. "Die Grabungsarbeiten des österreichischen
archäologischen Institutes in den Jahren 1924 bis
1929." JÖAI 26 (1930):294-312.

1155 _____. "Zur Geschichte der Bauten auf dem Ruinen-
feld der Marienkirche." In Forschungen in Ephesos.
vol. 4.1 Die Marienkirche in Ephesos. Vienna:
Benno Filser, 1932, pp. 1-12.

1156 Restle, Marcell. "Ephesos." In Reallexikon zur
byzantinischen Kunst. Edited by K. Wessel.
Stuttgart: Anton Hiersemann, 1971, 2:164-207.

1157 Reuer, Egon. "Zwei Zähne aus dem Sarkophag von
Belevi." In Forschungen in Ephesos. vol. 6 Das
Mausoleum von Belevi. Vienna: Österreichisches
Archäologisches Institut, 1979, pp. 201-02.

1158 de Ricci, Seymour. "Inscriptions concerning Diana of
the Ephesians." Proceedings of the Society of Biblical Archaeology 23 (1901):396-409.

1159 Richter, Gisela M. A. "Pliny's Five Amazons."
Archaeology 12 (1959):111-15.

1160 Ridgway, Brunilde S. "The Amazon's Belt: An
Addendum to a Story of Five Amazons." AJA 80
(1976):82.

1161 _____. "The Five Ephesian Amazons." In The
Proceedings of the Xth International Congress of
Classical Archaeology. Edited by E. Akurgal.
Ankara: Türk Tarih Kurumu Basimevi, 1978,
2:761-70.

1162 _____. "A Story of Five Amazons." AJA 78 (1974):
1-17.

1163 Riegl, Alois. "Oströmische Beiträge." In Beiträge
     zur Kunstgeschichte, Franz Wickhoff gewidmet.
     Vienna: A. Schroll and Co. 1903, pp. 1-11.

1164 Rigsby, Kent J. "The era of the province of Asia."
     Phoenix 33 (1979):39-47.

1165 Ritterling, Emil. "Zu zwei griechischen Inschriften
     römischer Verwaltungsbeamten." JÖAI 10 (1907):
     299-311.

     Robert, Jeanne. See nos. 393, 394.

1166 Robert, Jeanne and Louis. "Ephèse." REG Bull.
     Epig. 54 (1904):nos. 160-62.

1167 _____. "Ephèse." REG Bull. Epig. 56 (1942):no.
     151.

1168 _____. "Ephèse." REG Bull. Epig. 57 (1943):no.
     61.

1169 _____. "Ephèse." REG Bull. Epig. 58 (1944):nos.
     160-62.

1170 _____. "Ephèse." REG Bull. Epig. 60 (1946-1947):
     nos. 181-82.

1171 _____. "Ephèse." REG Bull. Epig. 61 (1948):no.
     206.

1172 _____. "Ephèse." REG Bull. Epig. 62 (1949):nos.
     150-53.

1173 _____. "Ephèse." REG Bull. Epig. 63 (1950):no.
     174.

1174 _____. "Ephèse." REG Bull. Epig. 64 (1951):nos.
     198-200.

1175 _____. "Ephèse." REG Bull. Epig. 65 (1952):no.
     141.

1176 _____. "Ephèse." REG Bull. Epig. 66 (1953):nos.
     176-79.

1177 _____. "Ephèse." <u>REG Bull. Epig.</u> 67 (1954):no. 219.

1178 _____. "Ephèse." <u>REG Bull. Epig.</u> 68 (1955):nos. 193-95.

1179 _____. "Ephèse." <u>REG Bull. Epig.</u> 71 (1958):nos. 421-22.

1180 _____. "Ephèse." <u>REG Bull. Epig.</u> 72 (1959):nos. 381-83.

1181 _____. "Ephèse." <u>REG Bull. Epig.</u> 73 (1960):nos. 346-47.

1182 _____. "Ephèse." <u>REG Bull. Epig.</u> 74 (1961):nos. 534-43.

1183 _____. "Ephèse." <u>REG Bull. Epig.</u> 75 (1962):nos. 284-86.

1184 _____. "Ephèse." <u>REG Bull. Epig.</u> 76 (1963):nos. 210-13.

1185 _____. "Ephèse." <u>REG Bull. Epig.</u> 77 (1964):no. 440.

1186 _____. "Ephèse." <u>REG Bull. Epig.</u> 78 (1965):nos. 340-43.

1187 _____. "Ephèse." <u>REG Bull. Epig.</u> 79 (1966):nos. 367-70.

1188 _____. "Ephèse." <u>REG Bull. Epig.</u> 80 (1967):nos. 495-520.

1189 _____. "Ephèse." <u>REG Bull. Epig.</u> 81 (1968):nos. 453-65.

1190 _____. "Ephèse." <u>REG Bull. Epig.</u> 82 (1969):nos. 508-12.

1191 _____. "Ephèse." <u>REG Bull. Epig.</u> 83 (1970):nos. 493-95.

1192 _____. "Ephèse." REG Bull. Epig. 84 (1971):nos. 567-80.

1193 _____. "Ephèse." REG Bull. Epig. 85 (1972):nos. 388-95.

1194 _____. "Ephèse." REG Bull. Epig. 86 (1973):nos. 379-82.

1195 _____. "Ephèse." REG Bull. Epig. 87 (1974):nos. 485-518.

1196 _____. "Ephèse." REG Bull. Epig. 89 (1976):nos. 595-602.

1197 _____. "Ephèse." REG Bull. Epig. 90 (1977):nos. 412-40.

1198 _____. "Ephèse." REG Bull. Epig. 91 (1978):nos. 414-29.

1199 _____. "Ephèse." REG Bull. Epig. 92 (1979):nos. 396-412.

1200 _____. "Ephèse." REG Bull. Epig. 93 (1980):nos. 444-56.

1201 _____. "Ephèse." REG Bull. Epig. 94 (1981):nos. 400-90.

1202 _____. "Ephèse." REG Bull. Epig. 95 (1982):nos. 294-318.

1203 _____. "Ephèse." REG Bull. Epig. 96 (1983):nos. 335-40.

1204 _____. "Ephèse." REG Bull. Epig. 97 (1984):nos. 369-74.

1205 _____. "Ephèse et la région." REG Bull. Epig. 69 (1956):nos. 253-56.

1206 _____. "Hiérocésarée." Hellenica 6 (1948):27-55.

1207 _____. "Métropolis d'Ionie." REG Bull. Epig. 95 (1982):no. 293.

1208 _____. "Stobi." REG Bull. Epig. 71 (1958):no. 303.

1209 Robert, Louis. "Actes d'affranchissement en Macédoine." Hellenica 1 (1940):70-77.

1210 _____. "Aphrodisias." Hellenica 13 (1965):119-25.

1211 _____. "Les 'bons jours du Stéphanéphore.'" Hellenica 3 (1946):77-78.

1212 _____. "Dans une maison d'Ephèse, un serpent et un chiffre." Comptes rendus de l'Académie des Inscriptions et Belles-Lettres (1982):126-32.

1213 _____. "La date de l'épigrammatiste Rufinus. Philologie et réalité." Comptes rendus de l'Académie des Inscriptions et Belles-Lettres (1982):50-63.

1214 _____. "Dedicaces et reliefs votifs." Hellenica 10 (1955):56-57; 86-89; 100-01; 156-57.

1215 _____. "En Ionie. l'Ephèse et l'émeri." In A Travers l'Asie Mineure. Poètes et prosateurs, monnaies grecques, voyageurs et géographie. Bibliothèque des Ecoles françaises d'Athènes et de Rome, 239. Athens: Ecole française d'Athènes, 1980, pp. 339-42.

1216 _____. "Epigrammes relatives à des gouverneurs." (Appendice: Un proconsul d'Asie au IVe siècle). Hellenica 4 (1948):35-114.

1217 _____. "Epitaphes juives d'Ephèse et de Nicomédie." Hellenica 11-12 (1960):381-413.

1218 _____. Etudes Anatoliennes. Recherches sur les inscriptions grecques de L'Asie Mineure. Etudes orientales, 5. Paris: E. de Boccard, 1937.

1219 _____. Etudes de numismatique grecque. Paris: Collège de France, 1951.

1220 _____. "Etudes d'épigraphie grecque. XXIX,

Sérapion d'Ephèse, trompette." Revue de philologie
4 (1930):49-53.

1221 _____ . "Les femmes théores à Ephèse." Comptes
rendus de l'Académie des Inscriptions et Belles-
Lettres (1974):176-81.

1222 _____ . Les gladiateurs dans l'Orient grec. Paris:
E. Champion, 1940.

1223 _____ . "Les hellénodiques à Ephèse." Hellenica
5 (1948):59-63.

1224 _____ . "Un monétaire à Ephèse." In Monnaies
grecques. Types, légendes, magistrats monétaires
et géographie. Hautes études numismatiques, 2.
Paris: Librairie Droz, 1967, p. 60.

1225 _____ . "Monnaies d'Ionie." Hellenica 7 (1949):
82-88.

1226 _____ . Monnaies grecques. Types, légendes,
magistrats monétaires et géographie. Hautes études
numismatiques, 2. Paris: Librairie Droz, 1967.

1227 _____ . "Monuments de gladiateurs dans l'Orient
grec." Hellenica 8 (1950):67-72.

1228 _____ . Noms indigènes dans l'Asie Mineure gréco-
romaine. Paris: Librairie Adrien Maisonneuve,
1963.

1229 _____ . "Le serpent Glycon d'Abônouteichos à
Athènes et Artémis d'Ephèse à Rome." Comptes
rendus de l'Académie des Inscriptions et Belles-
Lettres (1981):513-35.

1230 _____ . "Sur des inscriptions d'Ephèse, fêtes,
athlètes, empereurs, épigrammes." Revue de
philologie 41 (1967):7-84.

1231 _____ . "Sur des inscriptions d'Ephèse, XI. Sur
une lettre d'un proconsul d'Asie." Revue de
philologie 51 (1977):7-14.

1232 _____. "Sur des inscriptions d'Ephèse, XII."
Revue de philologie 55 (1981):9-13.

1233 _____. "Sur un décret d'Ephèse." Hellenica 3
(1946):79-85.

1234 _____. "Sur un décret des Korésiens au musée de
Smyrne." Hellenica 11-12 (1960):132-76.

1235 _____. "Sur une liste de Courètes à Ephèse."
Archaiologike Ephemeris (1967):129-36.

1236 _____. Villes d'Asie Mineure. Etudes de géographie
antique. 2nd ed. Paris: Editions E. de Boccard,
1962.

_____. See nos. 393, 394, 1166, 1167, 1168, 1169,
1170, 1171, 1172, 1173, 1174, 1175, 1176, 1177,
1178, 1179, 1180, 1181, 1182, 1183, 1184, 1185,
1186, 1187, 1188, 1189, 1190, 1191, 1192, 1193,
1194, 1195, 1196, 1197, 1198, 1199, 1200, 1201,
1202, 1203, 1204, 1205, 1206, 1207, 1208.

1237 Robert, Louis and Planhol, Xavier de. "Les inscriptions." In Laodicee du Lycos. Quebec: Presses
de l'Université Laval, 1969, pp. 247-389.

1238 Robinson, Edward S. G. "The Coins from the
Ephesian Artemision Reconsidered." Journal of
Hellenic Studies 71 (1951):156-67.

1239 _____. "The Date of the Earliest Coins." Numismatic Chronicle 6th ser. 16 (1956):1-8.

1240 Römer, E. "Das wiedererstehende Ephesus. Neue
Untersuchungen und Forschungen." Antiquitäten-
Rundschau 29 (1931):7-8.

1241 Roewer, Jan. Ephesos. Lebendige Vergangenheit.
Mit Texten von W. Alzinger and F. Hueber. Giessen: Mikado-Verlag, 1976.

1242 Rogers, Cleon L "The Dionysian Background of
Ephesians 5:18." Bibliotheca Sacra 136 (1979):
249-57.

1243 Rolland, H. "Sculptures antiques du Musée des Amis du vieux Toulon." Bulletin de la Société nationale des Antiquaires de France (1938):197-200.

1244 Romanelli, Pietro, and Guerrini, Lucia. "Efeso." In Enciclopedia dell'Arte Antica Classica e Orientale. Rome: Istituto Poligrafico dello Stato, 1960, 3:219-30.

1245 Roos, Paavo. "Wiederverwendete Startblöcke vom Stadion in Ephesos." JÖAI 52 (1978-1980):109-13.

Rosenbaum, Elisabeth. See no. 596.

1246 Rossner, Margarete. "Asiarchen und Archiereis Asias." Studii Clasice 16 (1974):101-42.

1247 Rostovtzeff, Mikhail I. [=Rostowzew] "Epiphaneiai." Klio 16 (1922):203-06.

1248 _____. The Social and Economic History of the Hellenistic World. Oxford: Clarendon Press, 1959.

1249 Roussel, P. "La vente de droit de cité (Note sur une inscription d'Ephèse)." Revue de philologie 37 (1963):332.

1250 Rozanova, N. P. "L'inscription dédiée à Artémis d'Ephèse trouvée à Panticapée en 1949" (in Russian). Vestnik Drevnej Istorii 73 (1961):130-32.

1251 Rylands, H., and Weber, G. "Description of the so-called Tomb of Saint Luke at Ephesus." Transactions of the Society of Biblical Archaeology 7 (1882):226-40.

1252- Saffrey, H. D. "Relire L'Apocalypse à Patmos."
53   Revue Biblique 82 (1975):410-17.

Sahin, Sencer. See nos. 926, 927, 966.

1254 Sakellarios, Michael B. "Symbole sten historia tou

phyletikou systematos tes Ephesou." Hellenika
(Athens) 15 (1957):220-31.

1255 Salditt-Trappmann, Regina. Tempel der ägyptischen
Götter in Griechenland und an der Westküste Kleinasiens. EPRO, 15. Leiden: E. J. Brill, 1970.

1256 Sallet, Alfred von. "Zum Neocorat der Ephesier."
Zeitschrift für Numismatik 1 (1874):278-85.

1257 Sande, Siri. "Zur Porträtplastik des sechsten nachrist-
lichen Jahrhunderts." Acta ad archaeologiam et
artis historiam pertinentia 6 (1975):65-108.

1258 Saporiti, Nada. "A Frieze from the Temple of Hadrian
at Ephesus." In Essays in Memory of Karl Lehmann.
Marsyas Supplement, 1. New York: New York University, 1964, pp. 269-78.

1259 Sartiaux, Félix. Villes mortes d'Asie Mineure.
Paris: Librairie Hachette et Cie, 1911, pp. 62-106.

1260 Sauer, Georg. "Ephesos und Petra. Beobachtungen
zur Stadtplanungen in hellenistischer Zeit." In
Lebendige Altertumswissenschaft. Festgabe zur
Vollendung des 70. Lebensjahres von Hermann Vetters dargebracht von Freunden, Schülern und Kollegen. Vienna: Verlag Adolf Holzhausen Nfg.,
1985, pp. 95-97.

1261 Schaber, Wilfried. Die archaischen Tempel der Artemis
von Ephesos. Entwurfsprinzipien und Rekonstruktion. Schriften aus dem Athenaion der Klassischen
Archäologie Salzburg, 2. Waldsassen: Stiftland-
Verlag, 1982.

1262 _____. "Rekonstruktion des Kroisostempels und des
Pythagorastempels in Ephesos." Dissertation, University of Salzburg, 1981.

1263 Schede, Martin. Antikes Traufleisten-Ornament.
Strassburg: J. H. Ed. Heitz, 1909, pp. 45; 64;
77-80; 85, 97; 106-9.

1264 Schindler, Anton. "Bemerkungen zur Karte." In

Forschungen in Ephesos. Vienna: Alfred Hölder,
1906, 1:235-36.

Schmitt, Rüdiger. See no. 427.

1265 Schmaltz, Bernhard. "Zum Sarkophag des Mausoleums
bei Belevi." JÖAI 49 (1968-1971):63-67.

1266 Schmitz, Leonhard. "Artemis." In A Dictionary of
Greek and Roman Biography and Mythology. Edited
by W. Smith. New York: AMS Press, 1967, 1:376.

1267 Schneider, Robert von. Ausstellung von Fundstücken
aus Ephesos im griechischen Tempel im Volksgarten.
Kunsthistorische Sammlungen des allerhöchsten
Kaiserhauses. Vienna: Adolf Holzhausen, 1901.

1268 _____. Ausstellung von Fundstücken aus Ephesos
im Unterem Belvedere. Kunsthistorische Sammlungen
des allerhöchsten Kaiserhauses. Vienna: Adolf
Holzhausen, 1905.

1269 _____. Ausstellung von Fundstücken aus Ephesos
im Unterem Belvedere. 2nd ed. Kunsthistorische
Sammlungen des allerhöchsten Kaiserhauses. Vienna:
Adolf Holzhausen, 1916.

1270 _____. Ausstellung von Fundstücken aus Ephesos
im Unterem Belvedere. 3rd ed. Kunsthistorische
Sammlungen des allerhöchsten Kaiserhauses. Vienna:
Adolf Holzhausen, 1919.

1271 Schönbauer, Ernst. "Drei interessante Inschriften aus
Ephesos." Iura. Rivista Internazionale di Diritto
Romano e Antico 16 (1965):105-115.

1272 Schreiber. "Artemis." In Ausführliches Lexikon der
griechischen und römischen Mythologie. Edited by
W. H. Roscher. Leipzig: B. G. Teubner, 1884-
1886, 1:588-93.

1273 Schreiber, Theodor. Apollon Pythoktonos. Ein Beitrag
zur griechischen Religions- und Kunstgeschichte.
Leipzig: W. Engelmann, 1879.

1274 Schulten, Adolf. "Zwei Erlässe des Kaisers Valens
      über die Provinz Asia." JÖAI 9 (1906):40-70.

1275 Schultze, Victor. "Ephesos." In Altchristliche Städte
      und Landschaften. II, Kleinasien pt. 2. Gütersloh:
      Evangelischer Verlag, 1926, pp. 86-120.

1276 Schwarz, Gerda. "Eine Priesterin aus Ephesos." In
      Classica et Provincialia. Festschrift für Erna Diez.
      Edited by G. Schwarz and E. Pochmarski. Graz:
      Akademische Druck und Verlagsanstalt, 1978, pp.
      183-88.

1277 Schwarz, Gerda, and Frel, Jiri. "Heraklit in Ephesos."
      The J. Paul Getty Museum Journal 5 (1977):161-74.

1278 Seibert, Jakob. "Die Schlacht bei Ephesos." Historia
      25 (1976):45-61.

1279 Seibt, Werner. "Drei byzantinische Bleisiegel aus
      Ephesos." In Litterae numismaticae Vindobonenses
      Roberto Goebl dedicatae. Vienna: Eckhel Club,
      1979, pp. 145-54.

1280 Seiterle, Gérard. "Artemis-Die Grosse Göttin von
      Ephesos." Antike Welt 10.3 (1979):3-16.

1281 _____. "Ephesos. Lysimachische Stadtmauer."
      JÖAI 47 (1964-1965):Grabungen 1966, 8-11.

1282 _____. "Das Hauptstadttor von Ephesos." Antike
      Kunst 25 (1982):145-49.

1283 _____. "Die hellenistische Stadtmauer von Ephesus."
      Dissertation, Zürich, 1970.

      Seiterle, S. See no. 342.

1284 Seltmann, Charles T. "The Earliest Hoarded Coins."
      Numismatic Circular 63 (1955):167.

1285 _____. Greek Coins. A History of Metallic Cur-
      rency and Coinage down to the Fall of the Hellen-
      istic Kingdoms. 2nd ed. London: Methuen, 1955.

1286 _____ . "Riot in Ephesus." In Riot in Ephesus. Writings on the heritage of Greece. London: Parrish, 1958.

1287 _____ . "The Wardrobe of Artemis." Numismatic Chronicle, 6th ser. 12 (1952):33-51.

1288 Senior. Ephèse ou Jérusalem. Ankara: Aydinlik, 1951.

1289 Seunig, G. Das ionische Kleinasien. I Teil. Ephesus. Triest: Verlag des K. K. Staats-Gymnasium, 1914.

Seze, Cevat. See no. 472.

1290 Sihler, E. G. "Some Notes on Ephesus." Theological Monthly 6 (1926):161-65; 199-203.

1291 Silverberg, Robert. The Seven Wonders of the Ancient World. New York: Crowell-Collier Press, 1970, pp. 60-75.

1292 Simpson, William. "The Supposed Tomb of St. Luke at Ephesos." Transactions of the Society of Biblical Archaeology 6 (1878):323-26.

1293 Smith, Arthur H. A Catalogue of sculpture in the Department of Greek and Roman antiquities, British Museum. Vol. 2, Part 6: The Sculptures of Ephesos, Cnidos, Cyrene and Salamis. London: William Clowes and Sons, 1900.

1294 _____ . "The Sculptures of the Croesus Temple." In Excavations at Ephesus. The Archaic Artemisia. Edited by D. G. Hogarth. London: Longmans and Co., 1908, pp. 293-312.

1295 Smith, Cecil. "The Ivory Statuettes." In Excavations at Ephesus. The Archaic Artemisia. Edited by D. G. Hogarth. London: Longmans and Co., 1908, pp. 155-85.

1296 _____ . "The Pottery." In Excavations at Ephesus. The Archaic Artemisia. Edited by D. G. Hogarth. London: Longmans and Co., 1908, pp. 218-31.

1297 Smith, Thomas. Remarks upon the manners, religion and government of the Turks, together with a survey of the Seven Churches of Asia, as they now lye in their ruines.... London: 1678.

1298 Sokolowski, Franciszek. Lois sacrées de l'Asie Mineure. Paris: E. de Boccard, 1955.

1299 _____. "A New Testimony of the Cult of Artemis of Ephesus." Harvard Theological Review 58 (1965): 427-31.

1300 Sotiriou, Georgios A. "Anaskaphai tou Byzantinou naou Ioannou tou Theologou en Epheso." Deltion 7 (1921-22):89-226.

1301 _____. "Anaskaphai tou Byzantinou naou tou Theologou en palaia Epheso." Praktika (1912):53-62.

1302- _____. "Grab und Kirche des hl. Johannes in der
03 Überlieferung und Bericht über die griech. Ausgrabung" (in Greek). In Forschungen in Ephesos. vol. 4.3 Die Johanneskirche. Vienna: Österreichisches Archäologisches Institut, 1951, pp. 5-13.

1304 _____. "Hellenikai anaskaphai en Mikra Asia. Ho naos Ioannou tou Theologou, en Epheso." Deltion 7 (1922-1924).

1305 Speidel, Michael P. "The Police Officer, a Hero. An Inscribed Relief from Near Ephesos." Epigraphica Anatolica 5 (1985):159-60.

1306 Squarciapino, M. "Medaglione Efesino di Commodo." Bulletino del Museo dell'impero Romano 12 (1941): 139-48.

1307 Stahr, Siegfried. "Ephesos-ein Beitrag Österreichs zur Paulusforschung." Theologisch-praktische Quartalschrift 110 (1962):193-208.

1308 Stein, Arthur. "Ephesische Ehreninschrift des Kaisers Nerva." JÖAI 2 (1899):Beibl. 71-74.

1309 Stengel. "Artemisia." Paulys Real-Encyclopädie der

classischen Altertumswissenschaft. Edited by G.
Wissowa. Stuttgart: J. B. Metzlerscher Verlag,
1896, 2:1442.

1310 _____. "Ephesia." Paulys Realencyclopädie der
klassischen Altertumswissenschaft. Edited by G.
Wissowa. Stuttgart: J. B. Metzlersche Buchhandlung, 1905, 5:2771.

1311 Stewart, A. F. "Lysippan Studies 3. Not by Daid-
alos?" AJA 82 (1978):473-82.

1312 Strocka, Volker M. "Efes'teki Celsus Kitapliği Onarim
Çalişmalari." Belleten 43 (1979):809-22.

1313 _____. "Ein ephesisches Urkundenrelief." JÖAI 49
(1968-71):41-49.

1314 _____. Forschungen in Ephesos, vol. 8.1 Die
Wandmalerei der Hanghäuser in Ephesos. Mit einem
Beitrag von Vetters, H. Vienna: Verlag der
Österreichischen Akademie der Wissenschaften,
1977.

1315 _____. "Die frühesten Girlandensarkophage. Zur
Kontinuität der Reliefsarkophage in Kleinasien
während des Hellenismus und der frühen Kaiserzeit." In Studien zur Religion und Kultur Kleinasien. Festschrift für Friedrich Karl Dörner zum
65. Geburtstag am 28. Februar 1976. Edited by
S. Şahin, E. Schwertheim, and J. Wagner. EPRO,
66.3. Leiden: E. J. Brill, 1978, 2:882-913.

1316 _____. "Neue archaische Löwen in Anatolien."
Archäologischer Anzeiger (1977):481-512.

1317 _____. "Römische Bibliotheken." Gymnasium 88
(1981):298-329.

1318 _____. "Theaterbilder aus Ephesos." Gymnasium
80 (1973):362-80.

1319 _____. "Wandmalerei." JÖAI 50 (1972-75):Grabun-
gen in Ephesos von 1960-1969 bzw. 1970, 469-94.

1320 _____. "Die Wandmalerei im römischen Ephesos."
In The Proceedings of the Xth International Congress
of Classical Archaeology. Edited by E. Akurgal.
Ankara: Türk Tarih Kurumu Basimevi, 1978, 1:481-
91.

1321 _____. "Zur Datierung der Celsusbibliothek." In
The Proceedings of the Xth International Congress
of Classical Archaeology. Edited by E. Akurgal.
Ankara: Türk Tarih Kurumu Basimevi, 1978, 2:893-
900.

1322 _____. "Zuviel Ehre für Scholastikia." In Lebendige Altertumswissenschaft. Festgabe zur Vollendung des 70. Lebensjahres von Hermann Vetters
dargebracht von Freunden, Schülern und Kollegen.
Vienna: Verlag Adolf Holzhausens Nfg., 1985, pp.
229-232.

_____. See no. 585.

1323 Strocka, Volker M., and Hueber, Friedmund. "Celsus
Kitapliği Fasadi restorasyonu." Efes Harabeleri ve
Müzesi Yilliği 1 (1972):97-98.

1324 _____. "Wiederaufbau der Fassade der Celsusbibliothek." Efes Harabeleri ve Müzesi Yilliği 1 (1972):
91-96.

1325 Strong, D. E. Catalogue of the Carved Amber in the
Department of Greek and Roman Antiquities. London: British Museum, 1966, pp. 41-6.

Strong, James. See no. 883.

1325a Strong, Mrs. S. A. (Eugenie). "Antiques in the Collection of Sir Frederick Cook, Bart., at Doughty
House, Richmond." Journal of Hellenic Studies 28
(1908):19-21.

1326 Stylianou, P. J. "Thucydides, the Panionian festival,
and the Ephesia (III 104) again." Historia 32 (1983):
245-49.

1327 Sutherland, Carol H. V. The Cistophori of Augustus.
London: The Royal Numismatic Society, 1970.

_____. See no. 880.

1328 Sutherland, Carol H. V., and Carson, Robert A. G.
The Roman Imperial Coinage. Revised edition.
London: Spink, 1984- .

1329 Svoronos, John N. "Ptolemais-Lebedos, Ephèse, Aenos
et Abdere sous les Ptolemées." Journal international d'Archéologie numismatique 5 (1902):61-70.

Swift, Louis J. See no. 1066.

1330 Sydenham, Edward A. The Coinage of the Roman Republic. London: Spink, 1952.

1331 Tanţău. Rodica. "Restudierea tezaurului de monede
romane republicane de la Stupini (jud. Bistriţa-
Năsăud)." Studii si Cercetari de Numismatică 5
(1971):255-64.

1332 Taylor, Lily R. "XXI. Artemis of Ephesus." In The
Beginnings of Christianity. Part I. Acts of the
Apostles. Edited by K. Lake and H. J. Cadbury.
Grand Rapids, Mich.: Baker Book House, reprinted
1979, 5:251-56.

1333 _____. "XXII. The Asiarchs." In The Beginnings
of Christianity. Part I. Acts of the Apostles.
Edited by K. Lake and H. J. Cadbury. Grand
Rapids: Baker Book House, reprinted 1979, 5:256-
62.

1334 Tek, Fikret. "1969-1970 Yili Domitianus Tapinaği
Kriptoportik Kazisinda Bulunan Kandiller." Efes
Harabeleri ve Müzesi Yilliği 1 (1972):36-42.

1335 Tersztyansky, J. "Morgendämmerung der griechischen
Münzprägung auf der kleinasiatischen Halbinsel."
Numizmatikai Közlöny 42 (1943):6-13.

1336 Theuer, Max. (+) "Das Bauwerk und seine Wieder-
herstellung." In Forschungen in Ephesos. vol. 6
Das Mausoleum von Belevi. Vienna: Österreichisches
Archäologisches Institut, 1979, pp. 11-72.

1337 _____. "Das Mausoleum bei Belevi." Vorträge anlässlich der 12. Tagung der Koldewey-Gesellschaft, no. 281.n.d., pp. 14-21.

_____. See nos. 1125, 1502.

1338 Thiersch, Hermann. Artemis Ephesia. Eine Archäologische Untersuchung. Abhandlungen der Gesellschaft der Wissenschaften zu Göttingen (Philologisch-historische Klasse) dritte Folge 12. Berlin: Weidmannsche Buchhandlung, 1935.

1339 _____. Ependytes und Ephod. Geisteswissenschaftliche Forschungen, 8. Stuttgart: Verlag W. Kohlhammer, 1936.

1340 Thür, Hilke, "Ephesische Bauhütten in der Zeit der Flavier und der Adoptivkaiser." In Lebendige Altertumswissenschaft. Festgabe zur Vollendung des 70. Lebensjahres von Hermann Vetters dargebracht von Freunden, Schülern und Kollegen. Vienna: Verlag Adolf Holzhausens, Nfg., 1985, pp. 181-87.

1341 Tierney, Michael. "Ephesus pagan and Christian." Studies, an Irish Quarterly Review 18 (1929):449-63.

1342 Toepffer. "Androkleidai." Paulys Real-Encyclopädie der classischen Altertumswissenschaft. Edited by G. Wissowa. Stuttgart: J. B. Metzlerscher Verlag, 1894, 1:2145-47.

1343 _____. "Androklos." Paulys Real-Encyclopädie der classischen Altertumswissenschaft. Edited by G. Wissowa. Stuttgart: J. B. Metzlerscher Verlag, 1894, 1:2147-48.

1344 Toksöz, Cemil. Ephesus Legends and Facts. Istanbul: Yenilik Basimevi, 1956.

1345 _____. Ephesus Legends and Facts. Ankara: Ayyildiz Matbaasi, 1962.

1346 _____. Ephesus Legends and Facts. Ankara: Ayyildiz Matbaasi, 1964.

1347 _____. Ephesus Legends and Facts. Ankara: Ayyildiz Matbaasi, 1967.

1348 _____. Ephesus Legends and Facts. Ankara: Ayyildiz Matbaasi, 1968.

1349 _____. Ephesus Legends and Facts. Anakra: Ayyildiz, 1969.

1350 _____. A travel guide to the historic treasures of Turkey. Istanbul: Alaş Ofset, 1977, pp. 167-81.

1351 Tonneau, Fr. Raphaël. "Ephèse au Temps de Saint Paul." Revue Biblique 38 (1929):5-34; 321-63.

1352 Tortorelli, Marisa G. "A Proposito dell'Artemis Efesia." Nuova rivista storica 56 (1972):440-52.

1353 Tourneur, Victor. "Monnaies grecques d'Asie, recueillies par M. Fr. Cumont." Revue Belge de Numismatique 69 (1913):109-37.

1354 Trell, Bluma L. "Architectura Numismatica Orientalis: A Short Guide to the Numismatic Formulae of Roman Syrian Die-Makers." Numismatic Chronicle 7th ser. 10 (1970):29-50.

1355 _____. "Architectura Numismatica: Part Two. Temples in Asia Minor." Dissertation, New York University, 1942.

1356 _____. "Contributions to Anatolian Temple Architecture." AJA 46 (1942):120.

1357 _____. "From the Temple of Diana of the Ephesians to the Chapel of the Holy Trinity in Washington Square." Arts and Sciences (Winter, 1965):10-16.

1358 _____. "A Further Study in Architectura Numismatica." AJA 67 (1963):218.

1359 _____. "A Further Study in Architectura Numismatica." In Essays in Memory of Karl Lehmann. Edited L. F. Sandler. Marsyas Supplement, 1.

New York: Institute of Fine Arts, New York University, 1964, pp. 384-98.

1360 _____. "A Link between the Medieval West and the pre-Greek East." In Congresso Internazionale di Numismatica Roma 11-16 settembre 1961, ii, Atti. Rome: Istituto Italiano di Numismatica, 1965, pp. 541-55.

1361 _____. "A Numismatic solution of two problems in Euripides." Numismatic Chronicle 7th ser. 4 (1964): 93-101.

1362 _____. "Prehellenic Sanctuaries on the Greco-roman coins of Anatolia." In The Proceedings of the Xth International Congress of Classical Archaology. Edited by E. Akurgal. Ankara: Türk Tarih Kurumu Basimevi, 1978, 1:107-20.

1363 _____. The Temple of Artemis at Ephesos. Numismatic Notes and Monographs, 107. New York: American Numismatic Society, 1945.

1364 _____. "Tomb, Altar or Shrine?" In Proceedings of the 8th International Congress of Numismatics. Edited by H. A. Cahn and G. Le Rider. Association internationale des numismates professionnels, 4. Paris: Bale, 1976, pp. 163-69.

_____. See no. 1127.

1365 Tretini, Johannes B. von. "Ephesos, oder wie der Jubilar einen interessierten Laien begeistert hat." In Lebendige Altertumswissenschaft. Festgabe zur Vollendung des 70. Lebensjahres von Hermann Vetters dargebracht von Freunden, Schülern und Kollegen. Vienna: Verlag Adolf Holzhausens Nfg., 1985, pp. xxvii-xxxi.

1365a Trombley, Frank R. "The Survival of Paganism in the Byzantine Empire During the Pre-Iconoclastic Period (540-727)." Dissertation, University of California, Los Angeles, 1981.

1366 Troxell, Hyla A. "Greek Accessions: Asia Minor to

India." American Numismatic Society Museum Notes 22 (1977):9-27.

1367 Tuchelt, Klaus. Frühe Denkmäler Roms in Kleinasien. Part 1, Roma und Promagistrate. Istanbuler Mitteilungen, Beiheft 23. Tübingen: Verlag Ernst Wasmuth, 1979.

1368 _____. "Pan und Pankult in Kleinasien." Istanbuler Mitteilungen 19-20 (1969-1970):223-36.

1369 Türkoğlu, Sabahattin. "Aysoluk (Selçuk, Ephesus), 1977. Recent Archaeological Research in Turkey." Anatolian Studies 28 (1978):13-14.

1370 _____. "Domitianus Kriptoportik'i Kazisinda Bulunan Portreler." Efes Harabeleri ve Müzesi Yilliği 1 (1972):15-31.

1371 _____. "Les Fouilles Du Crypto-Portique De Domitien." Efes Harabeleri ve Müzesi Yilliği 1 (1972): 12-14.

1372 _____. "Kuşadasi Tusan Oteli Yanindaki Kazi." Efes Harabeleri ve Müzesi Yilliği 1 (1972):84-90.

1373 _____. "Les Trois Portraits découverts devant la porte du Crypto-Portique du Temple de Domitien (résumé)." Efes Harabeleri ve Müzesi Yilliği 1 (1972):32-35.

1374 _____. "Les Trois Portraits trouvés à Ephèse." In The Proceedings of the Xth International Congress of Classical Archaeology. Edited by E. Akurgal. Ankara: Türk Tarih Kurumu Basimevi, 1978, 2:905-10.

1375 _____. "Yeni Efes Müzesi." Efes Müzesi Yilliği 2 (1973-1978):6-24.

_____. See no. 73.

1376 Türkoğlu, Sabahattin and Atalay, Erol. Efes Müzesi Rehberi. Izmir: Ticaret Matbaacilik, n.d.

1377 _____. "Efes'te Bulunan Hellenistik Porte
(Önrapor)." Türk Arkeoloji Dergisi 19.1 (1970):
213-15.

1378 Türkoğlu, Sabahattin and Meriç, Recep. "Domitian
Kriptoportiği Kazisi Ön Raporu." Efes Harabeleri
ve Müzesi Yilliği 1 (1972):5-11.

1379 Tüzün, Duygu. "Metropolis'ten Efes Müzesine gelen
Hellenistik Figürinler." Efes Müzesi Yilliği 2
(1973-1978):63-68.

1380 Vallois, René. "L'Artémision d'Ephèse: le 'temple' A;
les architectes du temple D." In Mélanges Gustav
Glotz. Paris: Presses Univ. de France, 1932,
2:839-50.

1380a Varinlioğlu, Ender. "Two Inscriptions from Ceramus."
ZPE 44 (1981):51-66.

1381 Vermeule, Cornelius C. "Dated Monuments of Hellenis-
tic and Graeco-Roman Popular Art in Asia Minor:
Ionia, Lydia and Phrygia." In Mélanges Mansel.
Türk Tarih Kurumu Yayinlari, Dizi 7, Sa. 60.
Ankara: Türk Tarih Kurumu Basimevi, 1974, 1:119-
26.

1382 _____. Roman Imperial Art in Greece and Asia
Minor. Cambridge: Harvard University Press,
1968.

1383 Verzone, Paolo. "Le fasi costruttive della basilica di
S. Giovanni Efeso." Rendiconti della Pontificia
Accademia di Archeologia 51-52 (1978-1980):213-35.

1384 _____. "Le grandi chiese a volta de VI secolo a
Constantinopoli, Efeso e Hierapolis." Corsi di
cultura sull'arte ravennate e bizantina 7 (1960):
133-40.

1385 _____. "S. Giovanni e S. Maria di Efeso e la
ricostruzione della citta nell'VIII secolo." Corsi di
cultura sull'arte ravennate e bizantina 12 (1965):
613-27.

1386 Vetters, Hermann. "Eine antike Grossstadt. Ephesos und seine Häuser." Die Baubude. Zeitschrift für die Mitarbeiter der HOCHTIEF 113 (June, 1984): 20-25.

1387 _____. "Die Arbeiten des österreichischen archäologischen Institutes in Ephesos/Belevi (1977)." Efes Müzesi Yilliği 2 (1973-1978):25-26.

1388 _____. "Die Ausgrabungen in Ephesos." Efes Harabeleri ve Müzesi Yilliği 1 (1972):4a-4d.

1389 _____. "Basilica Privata." In Classica et Provincialia. Festschrift für Erna Diez. Edited by G. Schwarz and E. Pochmarski. Graz: Akademische Druck und Verlagsanstalt, 1978, pp. 211-15.

1390 _____. Beiträge anlässlich der Gründung der Gesellschaft der Freunde von Ephesos am 10. April 1972.

1391 _____. "Bericht über die Ausgrabungen in den Jahren 1973-74." Türk Arkeoloji Dergisi 23.2 (1976):143-65.

1392 _____. "Bericht über die Ausgrabungen in Ephesos im Jahre 1970." Türk Arkeoloji Dergisi 19.2 (1970): 185-94.

1393 _____. "Bericht über die Ausgrabungen in Ephesos in den Jahren 1971-1972." Türk Arkeoloji Dergisi 22.1 (1975):127-40.

1394 _____. "Domitianterrasse und Domitiangasse." JÖAI 50 (1972-1975):Grabungen in Ephesos von 1960-1969 bzw. 1970, 311-30.

1395 _____. "Ephesos." In Wissenschaft und Weltbild, Festschrift für Hertha Firnberg, pp. 585-91, Vienna: Europaverlag, 1975.

1396 _____. "Ephesos, 1980." III. Kazi Sonuçlari Toplantisi (1981):77-79.

1397 _____. "Ephesos 1982." V. Kazi Sonuçlari Toplantisi (1983):261-63; 509-11.

1398 _____. "Ephesos, 1984." JÖAI 55 (1984):Beibl.

1399 _____. "Ephesos: Die Ergebnisse der Grabungen."
II. Kazi Sonuçlari Toplantisi (1980):85-6.

1400 _____. "Ephesus, 1969. Recent Archaeological
Research in Turkey." Anatolian Studies 20 (1970):
17.

1401 _____. "Ephesus, 1970. Recent Archaeological
Research in Turkey." Anatolian Studies 21 (1971):
37.

1402 _____. "Ephesos, 1971. Recent Archaeological
Research in Turkey." Anatolian Studies 22 (1972):
42-43.

1403 _____. "Ephesos, 1972. Recent Archaeological
Research in Turkey." Anatolian Studies 23 (1973):
35-36.

1404 _____. "Ephesos, 1973. Recent Archaeological
Research in Turkey." Anatolian Studies 24 (1974):
30-31.

1405 _____. "Ephesos, 1974. Recent Archaeological
Research in Turkey." Anatolian Studies 25 (1975):
24.

1406 _____. "Ephesos, 1975. Recent Archaeological
Research in Turkey." Anatolian Studies 26 (1976):
39-40.

1407 _____. "Ephesos, 1976. Recent Archaeological
Research in Turkey." Anatolian Studies 27 (1977):
38-39.

1408 _____. "Ephesos/Belevi, 1977. Recent Archaeological Research in Turkey." Anatolian Studies 28
(1978):20.

1409 _____. "Ephesos, 1978. Recent Archaeological
Research in Turkey." Anatolian Studies 29 (1979):
194-95.

1410 _____. "Ephesos, 1979. Recent Archaeological

Research in Turkey." Anatolian Studies 30 (1980): 211-13.

1411   . "Ephesos, 1980. Recent Archaeological Research in Turkey." Anatolian Studies 31 (1981): 184-86.

1412   . "Ephesus, 1982. Recent Archaeological Research in Turkey." Anatolian Studies 33 (1983): 241-42.

1413   . "Ephesus, 1983. Recent Archaeological Research in Turkey." Anatolian Studies 34 (1984): 213-14.

1414   . "Ephesus, 1984. Recent Archaeological Research in Turkey." Anatolian Studies 35 (1985): 191.

1415   . "Ephesos: Vorläufiger Grabungsbericht 1969." Anz. Wien 107 (1970):105-23.

1416   . "Ephesos: Vorläufiger Grabungsbericht 1970." Anz. Wien 108 (1971):85-101.

1417   . "Ephesos: Vorläufiger Grabungsbericht 1971." Anz. Wien 109 (1972):83-102.

1418   . "Ephesos: Vorläufiger Grabungsbericht 1972." Anz. Wien 110 (1973):175-94.

1419   . "Ephesos: Vorläufiger Grabungsbericht 1973." Anz. Wien 111 (1974):211-26.

1420   . "Ephesos: Vorläufiger Grabungsbericht 1975." Anz. Wien 113 (1976):493-507.

1421   . "Ephesos: Vorläufiger Grabungsbericht 1976." Anz. Wien 114 (1977):194-212.

1422   . "Ephesos: Vorläufiger Grabungsbericht 1977." Anz. Wien 115 (1978):263-74.

1423   . "Ephesos: Vorläufiger Grabungsbericht 1978." Anz. Wien 116 (1979):123-44.

1424 _____. "Ephesos: Vorläufiger Grabungsbericht 1979." Anz. Wien 117 (1980):249-66.

1425 _____. "Ephesos: Vorläufiger Grabungsbericht 1980." Anz. Wien 118 (1981):137-68.

1426 _____. "Ephesos: Vorläufiger Grabungsbericht 1981." Anz. Wien 119 (1982):62-101.

1427 _____. "Ephesos: Vorläufiger Grabungsbericht 1982." Anz. Wien 120 (1983):111-69.

1428 _____. "Ephesos: Vorläufiger Grabungsbericht 1983." Anz. Wien 121 (1984):209-32.

1429 _____. "Grabungen in Ephesos von 1960-1969 bzw. 1970." JÖAI 50 (1972-1975):Beibl. 225.

1430 _____. "Die Hanghäuser an der Kuretenstrasse." JÖAI 50 (1972-1975):Grabungen in Ephesos von 1960-1969 bzw. 1970, 331-80.

1431 _____. "Die Insulabauten in Ephesos." In Wohnungsbau im Altertum. Bericht über ein Kolloquium veranstaltet vom Architektur-Referat des Deutschen Archäologischen Instituts in Berlin vom 21.11 bis 23.11. 1978. Berlin: Wasmuth, 1978, pp. 197-98.

1432 _____. "75 Jahre Ausgrabungen in Ephesos." Wiener humanistische Blätter 14 (1972):5-9.

1433 _____. "Die Neapler 'Galleria' (zu Philostrat, Eikones I 4.)." JÖAI 50 (1972-1975):223-28.

1434 _____. "Neue römische Stockwerkbauten mit Wandmalereien in Ephesos." Antike Kunst 17 (1974):143-44.

1435 _____. "Neues von den Ausgrabungen in Ephesos." In VIII. Türk Tarih Kongresi. Türk Tarih Kurumu Yayinlari, 9.8. Ankara: Türk Tarih Kurumu Basimevi, 1979, 1:419-24.

1436 _____. "Nochmals zur Basilica Privata." In

Römische Historische Mitteilungen. (=Festgabe zur Hundert-Jahr-Feier der Gründung des Österreichischen Historischen Instituts in Rom) 23 (1981): 209-12.

1437 _____. "Die österreichischen Ausgrabungen in Ephesos 1969." Türk Arkeoloji Dergisi 18.2 (1969): 173-80.

1438 _____. "Der Schlangengott." In Studien zur Religion und Kultur Kleinasiens. Festschrift für Friedrich Karl Dörner zum 65. Geburtstag am 28. Februar 1976. Edited by S. Şahin, E. Schwertheim, and J. Wagner. EPRO, 66.2. Leiden: E. J. Brill, 1978, 2:967-79.

1439 _____. "Eine Standarte aus Ephesos." Istanbuler Mitteilungen 25 (1975):393-97.

1440 _____. "Ein Stuckraum in Ephesos." In Pro Arte Antiqua. Festschrift für Hedwig Kenner. 2: At Press. Sonderschriften herausgegeben vom Österreichischen Archäologischen Institut, 18. Vienna: Verlag A. F. Koska.

1441 _____. "Topographie und Geschichte von Ephesos." Festansprache: Die Arbeiten des ÖAI in Ephesos.

1442 _____. "Türkei/Ephesos." JÖAI 49 (1968-1971): Grabungen 1969, 7-21.

1443 _____. "Türkei/Ephesos." JÖAI 49 (1968-1971): Grabungen 1970, 3-19.

1444 _____. "Türkei/Ephesos." JÖAI 50 (1972-1974): Grabungen 1971-1972, 32-62.

1445 _____. "Türkei/Ephesos." JÖAI 51 (1976-1977): Grabungen 1973-1974, 20-26.

1446 _____. "Türkei/Ephesos 1982." JÖAI 54 (1983): Grabungen 1982, 28-34.

1447 _____. "Unternehmen Ephesos, Tätigkeitsbericht." Almanach Wien 123 (1973):221.

1448 _____. "Wachsen, Blühen und Vergehen: Ephesus."
Troja, Ephesus, Milet. Merian, Das Monatsheft der
Städte und Landschaften, 12.19. Hamburg: Hoff-
mann und Campe Verlag, 1966, pp. 32-37.

1449 _____. "Where St. Paul 'Fought with Beasts.'"
Part 1. "Continuing Excavations at Ephesus and
Roman Apartment-Houses Uncovered." Part II
"Frescoes and Statuary, Buildings Public and Pri-
vate, Recently Discovered in Ancient Ephesus."
Illustrated London News 244 (1964):766-68, 822-25.

1450 _____. "Zu römerzeitlichen Bauvorschriften." In
Forschungen und Funde-Festschrift Bernhard
Neutsch. Edited by F. Krinzinger, B. Otto, and E.
Walde-Psenner. Innsbrucker Beiträge zur Kulturwissenschaft, 21. Innsbruck: Institut für Sprachwissenschaft der Universität Innsbruck, 1980, pp.
477-85.

1451 _____. "Zum byzantinischen Ephesos." Jahrbuch
der Österreichischen Byzantinischen Gesellschaft
15 (1966):273-87.

1452 _____. "Zum Stockwerkbau in Ephesos." In
Mélanges Mansel. Türk Tarih Kurumu Yayinlari,
Dizi 7, Sa.60. Ankara: Türk Tarih Kurumu Basimevi,
1974, 1:69-91.

_____. See no. 778.

1453 Vetters, Hermann; Merkelbach, Reinhold; Knibbe,
Dieter; and Engelmann, Helmut. (Editors) Die
Inschriften von Ephesos. Inschriften griechischer
Städte aus Kleinasien. Bonn: Rudolf Habelt, 1979-
1984, 8 volumes.

1454 _____. "Ein Repertorium der Inschriften von
Ephesos." ZPE 26 (1977):94.

1455 Vetters, Wolfgang. "Die Küstenverschiebungen
Kleinasien: eine Konsequenz tektonischer Ursachen."
In Lebendige Altertumswissenschaft. Festgabe zur
Vollendung des 70. Lebensjahres von Hermann

Vetters dargebracht von Freunden, Schülern und Kollegen. Vienna: Verlag Adolf Holzhausens Nfg., 1985, pp. 33-37.

1456 Visser, Marinus Willem de. Die nicht menschengestaltigen Götter der Griechen. Leiden: E. J. Brill, 1903.

1457 Voigtländer, Walter. Der jüngste Apollontempel von Didyma. Geschichte seines Baudekors. Istanbuler Mitteilungen, Beiheft 14. Tübingen: Verlag Ernst Wasmuth, 1975.

1458 Volk, Otto; Emminghaus, Johannes H.; and Baus, Karl. "Ephesos." In Lexikon für Theologie und Kirche. 2nd ed. Edited by J. Höfer and K. Rahner. Freiburg: Verlag Herder, 1959, 3:919-23.

Vos, Howard F. See no. 1088.

1459 Wace, Alan J. B. "Recent excavations in Asia Minor. Ephesus." Journal of Hellenic Studies 23 (1903): 340-50.

1460 Waddington, William Henry. Recueil général des monnaies grecques d'Asie Mineure. Paris: E. Leroux, 1904.

_____. See no. 825.

1461 Waele, F. J. de "Ephesos, stad von de Moedergodin en van de Moeder Gods." 't Heilig Land (Nijmegen) (1958):148-60.

1462 Wagenvoort, H. "Inspiratie door bijen in de droom." Mededelingen der Koninklijke Nederlandse Akademie van Wetenschappen, n.r. 29, no. 8 (1966):263-72.

Waldbaum, Jane C. See no. 487.

1463 Wankel, Hermann. "Die Bekanntmachung des Todesurteils in der ephesischen Inschrift Inv. 1631." ZPE 24 (1977):219-21.

1464 _____. Inschriften griechischer Städte aus Kleinasien. XI: Die Inschriften von Ephesos. 1,a:
Nr. 1-47 (Texte). Bonn: Habelt, 1979.

1465 _____. "Zu dem ephesischen Opfergesetz Inv. 1273
(=Sokolowski Suppl. 121)." ZPE 29 (1978):51-53.

1466 Warnecke, B. "Antiskenos des ephesischen Theaters."
Philologus n.f. 35 (1925-1926):127-8.

1467 Waser, Otto. "Demos, die Personifikation des Volkes."
Revue Suisse Numismatique 7 (1898):313-35.

1468 Weber, Ekkehard. "Eine unbekannte Bezeichnung für
eine wichtige Tätigkeit im Schiffsbau." ZPE 13
(1974):18-20.

1469 Weber, G. "Description of the so-called tomb of St.
Luke at Ephesus. With Notes by W. H. Rylands."
Transactions of the Society of Biblical Archaeology
7 (1882):226-40.

1470 _____. "Etude sur la chorographie d'Ephèse."
Mouseion kai Bibliotheke tes [en Smyrne] Euangelikes Scholes. (1880-1884):1-44.

1471 _____. Guide du voyageur à Ephèse. Smyrne: La
Presse, 1891.

1472 _____. "Un monument circulaire à Ephèse ou
prétendu Tombeau de saint Luc." Revue archéologique 3rd ser. 17 (1891):36-48.

1473 _____. "Tumulus et hieron de Bélévi sur l'ancienne
route d'Ephèse à Sardes." Mouseion kai Bibliotheke
tes [en Smyrne] Euangelikes Scholes. (1878-1880):
89-104.

_____. See no. 1251.

1474 Weber, Leo. "Apollon Pythoktonos im phrygischen
Hierapolis." Philologus 69 (1910):178-251.

1475 _____. "Die Homoniemünzen des phrygischen
Hierapolis. Ein Beitrag zur Erklärung der Homonie."

Journal international d'Archéologie numismatique 14 (1912):65-122.

1476 Weber, Martha. "Die Amazonen von Ephesos." Jahrbuch des Deutschen Archäologischen Instituts 91 (1976):28-96.

1477 Wegner, Max. "Gewundene Säulen von Ephesos." JÖAI 51 (1976-1977):Beibl. 49-64.

1478 _____. "Soffitten von Ephesos und Asia Minor." JÖAI 52 (1978-1980):91-107.

1479 _____. "Zwei oströmische Bildwerke." Kleinasien und Byzanz. Gesammelte Aufsätze zur Altertumskunde und Kuntsgeschichte. Istanbuler Forschungen, 17. Berlin: Walter de Gruyter & Co., 1950, pp. 159-61.

1480 Weidauer, Liselotte. "Die Elektronprägung in der orientalisierenden Epoche frühgriechischer Kunst." Schweizerische numismatische Rundschau 60 (1981): 7-25.

1481 _____. Probleme der frühen Elektronprägung. Typos. Monographien zur antiken Numismatik, 1. Fribourg: Office du Livre, 1975.

1482 Weigand, Edmund. "Propylon und Bogentor in der östlichen Reichskunst, ausgehend vom Mithridatestor in Ephesos." Wiener Jahrbuch für Kunstgeschichte 5 (1928):71-114.

1483 Weiss, Egon. "Zum Stadtrecht von Ephesos." JÖAI 18 (1915):Beibl. 285-306.

1484 Weiss, Peter. "Zu dem neuen Graffito-Epigramm aus Ephesus." Chiron 3 (1973):451-55.

1485 Weisshäupl, Rudolf. "Ephesische Latrinen-Inschriften." JÖAI 5 (1902):Beibl. 33-34.

1486 Wendel, Clarence A. "Land Tilting or Silting? Which Ruined Ancient Aegean Harbors?" Archaeology 22 (1969):322-24.

1487 Weninger, Josef. "Ein Schädel aus einem ephesischen
     Heroengrab aus der Zeit um Christi Geburt." In
     Festschrift für Rudolf Egger. Beiträge zur älteren
     Europäischen Kultur Geschichte. Klagenfurt: Ver-
     lag des Geschichtsvereines für Kärnten, 1953,
     2:158-68.

1488 Werner, Ernst, and Werner, Hilde. "Die Restaurierung
     des Stuckgewölbes im Hanghaus 2 in Ephesos." In
     Lebendige Altertumswissenschaft. Festgabe zur
     Vollendung des 70. Lebensjahres von Hermann Vet-
     ters dargebracht von Freunden, Schülern und Kol-
     legen. Vienna: Verlag Adolf Holzhausens Nfg.,
     1985, pp. 399-402.

     Werner, Hilde. See no. 1488.

1489 Wernicke. "Artemis." Paulys Real-Encyclopädie der
     classischen Altertumswissenschaft. Edited by G.
     Wissowa. Stuttgart: J. B. Metzlerscher Verlag,
     1896, 2:1372-73; 1385-86.

1490 Wesenberg, Burkhardt. "Agesilaos im Artemision."
     ZPE 41 (1981):175-80.

1491 "Die Wiederauffindung des Johannesgrabes in
     Ephesus." Biblica 13 (1932):121-24.

1492 Wiegartz, Hans. Kleinasiatische Säulensarkophage.
     Untersuchungen zum Sarkophagtypus und zu den
     figürlichen Darstellungen. Istanbuler Forschungen,
     26. Berlin: Verlag Gebr. Mann, 1965.

1493 _____. "Zu den Columnae Caelatae des jüngeren
     Artemision." Marburger Winckelmann-Programm
     (1968):41-73.

1494 Wikenhauser, Alfred. Die Apostelgeschichte und ihr
     Geschichtswert. Neutestamentiche Abhandlungen,
     8. Münster: Verlag der Aschendorffschen Verlags-
     buchhandlung, 1921, pp. 342-43; 363-69.

1495 Wilberg, Wilhelm. "Das Brunnenhaus am Theater." In
     Forschungen in Ephesos. Vienna: Österreichische
     Verlagsgesellschaft, 1923, 3:266-73.

1496 _____. "Die Fassade der Bibliothek in Ephesus."
JÖAI 11 (1908):118-35.

1497 _____. "Stierkopfkapitell aus Ephesos." JÖAI 12
(1909):207-14.

_____. See no. 153, 519.

1498 Wilberg, Wilhelm, and Heberdey, Rudolf. "Der
Aquädukt des C. Sextilius Polio." In Forschungen
in Ephesos. Vienna: Österreichische Verlagsgesellschaft, 1923, 3:256-65.

1499 _____. "Die Viersäulenbau auf dem Arkadiane-
strasse." In Forschungen in Ephesos. Vienna:
Alfred Hölder, 1906, 1:132-42.

1500 Wilberg, Wilhelm and Keil, Josef. "Die Agora." In
Forschungen in Ephesos. Vienna: Österreichische
Verlagsgesellschaft, 1923, 3:1-168.

1501 Wilberg, Wilhelm; Niemann, George; and Heberdey,
Rudolf. "Torbauten am Hafen." In Forschungen
in Ephesos. Vienna: Österreichische Verlagsgesellschaft, 1923, 3:169-223.

1502 Wilberg, Wilhelm; Theuer, Max; Keil, Josef; and
Eichler, Fritz. Forschungen in Ephesos. 5.1
Celsusbibliothek. Vienna: Österreichische
Verlagsgesellschaft, 1944.

1503 Wilhelm, Adolf. "Dapsiles." In Festschrift zum 70.
Geburtstag von Paul Kretschmer. Göttingen:
Vandenhoeck and Ruprecht, 1936, pp. 269-73
[=Glotta. Zeitschrift für griechische und
lateinische Sprache, 25].

1504 _____. "Zu einer Inschrift aus Ephesos."
Rheinisches Museum für Philologie 77 (1928):180-81.

1505 Willemsen, Franz. "Aktaionbilder." Jahrbuch des
Deutschen Archäologischen Instituts 71 (1956):29-58.

1506 Windham, J. "On a passage in Pliny's N. H. relative
to the temple of Diana at Ephesos (1779)."
Archaeologia 6 (1782):65-75.

1507 Winer, Georg B. "Ephesus." In Biblisches Realwör-
       terbuch zum Handgebrauch. 2nd ed. Edited by
       G. B. Winer. Leipzig: Carl Heinrich Reclam, 1833.

1508 Winter, Erich. "Eine ägyptische Bronze aus Ephesos."
       Zeitschrift für ägyptische Sprache und Altertums-
       kunde 97 (1971):146-55.

1509 Winter, Frederick. E. "Toward a Chronology of the
       Later Artemision at Ephesos." AJA 84 (1980):241.

1509a Wiplinger, Gilbert. "Hanghaus-Konservierungsprojekt
       1983." Anz. Wien 121 (1984):226-29.

1510- _____. "Neues zum Hof H2/SR27 des Hanghauses 2
   11   von Ephesos." In Lebendige Altertumswissenschaft.
       Festgabe zur Vollendung des 70. Lebensjahres von
       Hermann Vetters dargebracht von Freunden,
       Schülern und Kollegen. Vienna: Verlag Adolf
       Holzhausens Nfg., 1985, pp. 204-08.

1512 _____. "Sicherung der Ruinen des Hanghauses an
       der Kuretenstrasse in Ephesos." Master's Thesis.
       Technical University of Vienna, 1978.

1513 _____. "Zum Hanghausprojekt in Ephesos." JÖAI
       56 (1985):83-91.

1514 Wittek, Paul. Das Fürstentum Mentesche. Studie zur
       Geschichte Westkleinasiens im 13.-15. Jh. Istan-
       buler Mitteilungen, 2. Istanbul: Universum
       Druckerei, 1934.

1515 Wittich, H. "Über den Tempel des didymäischen Apollo
       bei Milet und den der Diana von Ephesus in metro-
       logischer Beziehung." Archäologische Zeitung 16
       (1858):144-8.

1516 _____. "Zum ephesischen Artemision." Archäo-
       logische Zeitung 30 (1873):29-31.

1517 Wörrle, Michael. "Ägyptisches Getreide für Ephesos."
       Chiron 1 (1971):325-40.

1518 _____. "Zur Datierung des Hadrianstempels an der

'Kuretenstrasse' in Ephesos." Archäologischer Anzeiger 88 (1973):470-77.

Wolff, Petra. See no. 131.

1519 Wolters, Paul. "Archiatros to d'." JÖAI 9 (1906): 295-97.

1520 Wood, John T. Discoveries at Ephesus, Including the Sites and Remains of the Great Temple of Diana. Boston: James R. Osgood & Co., 1877.

1521 _____. (+). Modern Discoveries on the Site of Ancient Ephesus. By-Paths of Bible Knowledge, 14. London: Religious Tract Society, 1890.

1522 _____. "On the Antiquities of Ephesus having Relation to Christianity." Transactions of the Society of Biblical Archaeology 6 (1878):327-33.

1523 _____. "Reply to Mr. Fergusson's Paper 1882-83 on the Temple of Diana at Ephesus." Transactions of the Royal Institute of British Architects (1883-1884): 165-70.

_____. See no. 385.

1524 Woodward, A. M. "Archaeology in Greece, 1926-27." Journal of Hellenic Studies 47 (1927):260-61.

1525 _____. "Notes on the Augustan cistophori." Numismatic Chronicle 6th ser. 12 (1952):19-32.

1526 Wotschitzky, Alfons. "Ephesos. Past, Present and Future of an Ancient Metropolis." Archaeology 14 (1961):205-12.

1527 Wulf, Berthold. Athen und Ephesus; von der Geburt des Christentums und der Seele Griechenlands. Freiburg: Die Kommenden, 1978.

1528 Yalouri, Athanasia. "A Hero's Departure." AJA 75 (1971):269-75.

1529 Yamauchi, Edwin. The Archaeology of New Testament
      Cities in Western Asia Minor. Grand Rapids:
      Baker Book House, 1980, pp. 79-114.

1530 _____. "Ramsay's Views on Archaeology in Asia
      Minor Reviewed." In The New Testament Student
      and his Field. The New Testament Student, 5.
      Edited by J. H. Skilton. Phillipsburg, NJ: Pres-
      byterian and Reformed Publishing Co., 1982, pp.
      27-40.

1531 Young, R. S. "Doodling at Gordion." Archaeology
      22 (1969):270-75.

1532 Ziebarth, Erich. "Zum griechischen Schulwesen."
      JÖAI 13 (1910):108-16.

1533 Zimmermann, Gustav A. Ephesos im ersten christlichen
      Jahrhundert. Ein Beitrag zur neutestamentlichen
      Zeitgeschichte. Leipzig: Druck von F. A. Brock-
      haus, 1874.

1534 Zschietzschmann, Willy. "Ephesos." In Der Kleine
      Pauly Lexikon der Antike. Edited by K. Ziegler
      and W. Sontheimer. Munich: Deutscher Taschen-
      buch Verlag, 1975, 2:293-96.

1535 Žužić, Marko. A Short History of St. John in Ephesus.
      Limo, Ohio: The American Society of Ephesus,
      1960.

SUBJECT INDEX

AGORA 6, 7, 8, 9, 10, 11, 12, 26, 30, 31, 37, 38, 138,
    207, 294, 371, 374, 417, 504, 505, 507, 510, 511, 514,
    555, 582, 621, 683, 684, 685, 717, 747, 748, 808, 809,
    873, 1014, 1057, 1058, 1259, 1350, 1351, 1416, 1422,
    1423, 1424, 1426, 1427, 1428, 1500, 1529; see also
    STATE AGORA
ALEXANDER THE GREAT 38, 207, 345a, 1069
AMAZONS 30, 38, 89, 96, 99a, 132, 133, 154, 163, 172,
    207, 274, 275, 285, 321, 330, 331, 441, 473, 509, 561,
    588, 764, 799, 1039, 1097, 1098, 1159, 1160, 1161,
    1162, 1258, 1476
ANDROKLOS 38, 132, 207, 325, 426, 473, 644, 646, 718,
    837, 1009, 1069, 1134, 1258, 1342, 1343, 1500
APHRODITE 38, 65, 132, 207, 319, 395, 397, 406, 473,
    659, 746, 818, 875, 1069
APOLLO 30, 38, 132, 207, 473, 491, 594, 609, 644, 707,
    746, 1069, 1230, 1273
APOLLONIUS OF TYANA 207, 1069; see also PHILOSOPHY,
    RHETORIC, AND EDUCATION
ARCHITECTURE 7, 8, 9, 10, 11, 12, 20, 21, 25, 26, 27,
    28, 30, 32, 33, 35, 37, 38, 39, 40, 47, 48, 49, 72, 94,
    95, 96, 97, 98, 99, 99a, 100, 101, 102, 103, 104, 106,
    108, 111, 112, 113, 114, 119, 120, 125, 127, 129, 130,
    132, 133, 143, 152, 178, 187, 188, 196, 207, 235, 245,
    250, 256, 259, 289, 293, 295, 303, 343, 370, 371, 374,
    375, 376, 378, 381, 382, 383, 384, 385, 403, 413, 417,
    420, 421, 422, 423, 432, 443, 446, 449, 475, 476, 485,
    498, 499, 512, 513, 514, 515, 519, 525, 526, 527, 528,
    541, 544, 546, 547, 548, 549, 552, 553, 554, 555, 557,
    558, 563, 568, 569, 572, 578, 579, 580, 581, 582, 583,
    584, 585, 586, 606, 611, 612, 620, 621, 623, 625, 625a,
    631, 651, 652, 653, 654, 711, 742, 748, 764, 780, 781,
    794, 795, 796, 808, 809, 833, 838, 839, 840, 841, 842,
    843, 844, 845, 846, 847, 859, 860, 861, 865, 977,
    1006, 1022, 1027, 1028, 1029, 1036, 1051, 1055, 1062,
    1067, 1069, 1072, 1076, 1097, 1101, 1102, 1103, 1105,

140, 143, 152, 153, 172, 192, 193, 207, 214, 226, 235,
245, 250, 256, 258, 293, 294, 312, 329, 330, 331, 343,
345a, 370, 371, 381, 382, 383, 384, 385, 388, 389, 390,
406, 417, 426, 438, 439, 441, 446, 460, 462, 466, 485,
487, 500, 523, 524, 525, 526, 527, 528, 531, 533, 533a,
537, 556, 557, 558, 559, 560, 561, 562, 563, 564, 565,
566, 567, 568, 569, 572, 577, 586, 589a, 594, 600, 621,
628, 630, 639, 640, 642, 644, 683, 684, 685, 748, 768,
769, 780, 782, 793, 794, 795, 796, 798, 799, 800, 801,
807, 822, 828, 837, 838, 839, 840, 841, 842, 843, 844,
845, 846, 847, 850, 855, 859, 860, 861, 871, 873, 880a,
1014, 1027, 1028, 1029, 1055, 1057, 1058, 1063, 1068,
1069, 1070, 1071, 1076, 1078, 1082, 1095, 1097, 1099,
1101, 1102, 1103, 1105, 1110, 1111, 1117, 1118, 1127,
1129, 1131, 1140, 1146, 1213, 1215, 1230, 1238, 1239,
1241, 1259, 1261, 1262, 1263, 1280, 1286, 1287, 1291,
1293, 1294, 1295, 1296, 1298, 1299, 1338, 1344, 1345,
1346, 1347, 1348, 1349, 1350, 1351, 1354, 1356, 1357,
1358, 1359, 1360, 1361, 1362, 1363, 1380, 1415, 1416,
1417, 1418, 1419, 1420, 1421, 1422, 1424, 1425, 1426,
1427, 1435, 1456, 1463, 1470, 1481, 1483, 1489, 1490,
1493, 1494, 1506, 1509, 1515, 1516, 1523, 1529
ASCLEPIUS 132, 207, 644, 717, 718, 722, 745, 746, 1069,
1418, 1422
ASIARCHATE AND KOINON 207, 417, 481, 533, 577, 598,
644, 727, 744, 745, 747, 752, 754, 755, 756, 764, 850,
855, 856, 867, 883, 962, 1021, 1026, 1070, 1140, 1246,
1333, 1494, 1500, 1529, 1533
ASYLUM 26, 152, 157, 207, 258, 561, 644, 748, 867, 1068,
1069, 1206, 1313, 1489, 1529; see also ARTEMISION
ATHENA 38, 78, 132, 152, 207, 406, 644, 729, 745, 746,
852, 1069
ATTIS 38, 132, 641, 645, 649, 1069
AUDITORIUM 30, 37, 38, 499, 510, 511, 512, 522, 585, 613,
683, 684, 685, 722, 1057, 1421, 1422, 1427, 1428, 1500,
1529; see also EMBOLOS; CELSUS LIBRARY
AYASOLUK HILL 7, 8, 9, 10, 11, 12, 30, 37, 38, 91, 152,
207, 417, 837, 1037, 1134, 1344, 1345, 1346, 1347,
1348, 1349, 1470

BANKING AND ECONOMICS 55, 74, 100, 152, 176, 197, 199,
207, 258, 345a, 417, 454, 564, 629, 644, 720, 745, 764,
769, 820, 867, 939, 946, 1064, 1065, 1068, 1069, 1070,
1097, 1248, 1483, 1489, 1529

EXCAVATION REPORTS (ANNUAL) 18, 22, 144, 145, 151,
    236, 237, 238, 261, 262, 264, 265, 266, 310, 311, 312,
    313, 314, 315, 316, 323, 324, 325, 326, 327, 328, 329,
    330, 331, 334, 335, 336, 337, 342, 498, 499, 502, 505,
    506, 507, 508, 509, 510, 511, 512, 513, 514, 515, 650,
    664, 716, 717, 718, 719, 720, 721, 722, 723, 724, 731,
    890, 891, 892, 893, 894, 895, 896, 897, 898, 899, 900,
    901, 902, 903, 904, 905, 906, 907, 908, 909, 910, 911,
    912, 913, 914, 915, 981, 982, 983, 984, 989, 990, 992,
    993, 995, 1000, 1002, 1006, 1007, 1008, 1009, 1010,
    1013, 1153, 1154, 1387, 1388, 1391, 1392, 1393, 1396,
    1397, 1398, 1399, 1400, 1401, 1402, 1403, 1404, 1405,
    1406, 1407, 1408, 1409, 1410, 1411, 1412, 1413, 1414,
    1415, 1416, 1417, 1418, 1419, 1420, 1421, 1422, 1423,
    1424, 1425, 1426, 1427, 1428, 1429, 1437, 1442, 1443,
    1444, 1445, 1446
EXCAVATIONS, HISTORY AND SUMMARY OF 30, 37, 38,
    80, 81, 82, 83, 84, 85, 86, 92, 113, 124, 138, 139,
    140, 141, 207, 219, 226, 247, 318, 343, 345a, 364, 365,
    367, 371, 374, 390, 406, 417, 458, 519, 532, 557, 558,
    568, 569, 574, 585, 621, 623, 630, 644, 660, 662, 663,
    664, 665, 666, 667, 668, 673, 676, 679, 680, 681, 682,
    683, 684, 685, 689, 691, 705, 706, 760, 778, 787, 788,
    789, 806, 810, 812, 872, 980, 985, 987, 988, 998, 1001,
    1005, 1013, 1034, 1055, 1059, 1073, 1074, 1078, 1129,
    1153, 1154, 1240, 1241, 1244, 1300, 1302, 1341, 1351,
    1369, 1387, 1388, 1390, 1394, 1395, 1432, 1435, 1447,
    1448, 1449, 1459, 1500, 1520, 1521, 1522, 1524, 1526,
    1529

FORTIFICATION AND WALLS 7, 8, 9, 10, 11, 12, 26, 30,
    37, 38, 111, 138, 152, 207, 329, 345a, 371, 417, 574,
    610, 683, 684, 685, 716, 868, 876, 972, 1057, 1156,
    1241, 1281, 1283, 1421, 1422, 1423, 1425, 1426, 1427
FOUNTAINS, AQUEDUCTS, AND WELLS 7, 8, 9, 10, 11, 12,
    26, 30, 37, 38, 47, 48, 49, 77a, 106, 108, 132, 138,
    152, 207, 294, 326, 327, 328, 345a, 360, 371, 391, 395,
    406, 410, 413, 417, 422, 423, 485, 512, 514, 515, 631,
    644, 673, 683, 684, 685, 711, 717, 749, 764, 771, 772,
    810, 950, 1002, 1009, 1010, 1014, 1057, 1058, 1067,
    1156, 1340, 1350, 1385, 1415, 1416, 1419, 1424, 1425,
    1426, 1427, 1428, 1495, 1498